HANDBOOK OF PAINTINGS

The Frick
Collection

Handbook
of
Paintings

NEW YORK · 1971

Cover illustrations:

Details from *St. Francis in Ecstasy*

Giovanni Bellini (c. 1430-1516)

PREFACE

This *Handbook of Paintings* is planned primarily for the use of visitors while viewing the pictures in the galleries of The Frick Collection. In function it thus replaces the small handbooks and summary catalogues issued before the publication of *The Frick Collection: An Illustrated Catalogue*. For the most recent and complete information on each of the paintings, the reader is referred to Volumes I and II of this *Catalogue*, published in 1968.*

The entries in the *Handbook* are ultimately based on the *Illustrated Catalogue of the Works of Art in the Collection of Henry Clay Frick* (1949-56), published and privately distributed by The Frick Art Reference Library. Edgar Munhall, Curator, prepared the text of the *Handbook*, with the assistance of Bernice Davidson, Research Curator. Jethro Hurt and John Walsh contributed to the entries for Flemish and Dutch paintings. The text was edited by Joseph Focarino.

The *Handbook* was designed by Joseph Blumenthal in cooperation with the staff of The Frick Collection, and was printed by The Spiral Press.

H. D. M. G.

*The nine-volume *Catalogue* is distributed by Princeton University Press.

EXPLANATORY NOTE

AUTHORSHIP: For the few paintings that cannot with certainty be attributed to specific artists, the following classifications are used: *Workshop of* (implying that the design may have been the master's but the execution was, in part at least, by an assistant); *Circle of* (implying that the unidentified artist probably had been trained by the master or influenced by close connection with him); and *Follower of* (implying that the unknown artist imitated the master's style but may have had no direct contact with him).

DIMENSIONS: Measurements represent stretcher or panel size. Height precedes width.

HISTORICAL NOTE

THE Frick Collection was founded by Henry Clay Frick (1849-1919), the Pittsburgh coke and steel industrialist. At his death Mr. Frick bequeathed his New York residence and the finest of his works of art to establish a public gallery of art for the purpose of "encouraging and developing the study of the fine arts." Among the numerous works bequeathed by Mr. Frick were one hundred thirty-one paintings. Since that time thirty-eight additional paintings have been purchased by the Trustees from an endowment provided by Mr. Frick.

Mr. Frick grew up in the vicinity of Pittsburgh. From an early age he was interested in art, and his acquisitions recorded over a span of forty years show a continuing development of interest and taste. After initially collecting Salon pictures and paintings of the Barbizon School, he purchased his first old masters around the turn of the century, and in the next decade he acquired many of the outstanding paintings that established the character of the Collection as viewed today. An extended account of Mr. Frick's collecting is included in the biographical essay "Henry Clay Frick, Art Collector," which appears as an introduction to Volume I of *The Frick Collection: An Illustrated Catalogue.*

BARNA DA SIENA   Active around 1350

Though little is known of the life of Barna, his frescoes in the Collegiata at San Gimignano firmly establish him as the leading Sienese painter in the second half of the fourteenth century.

Christ Bearing the Cross, with a Dominican Friar   (27.1.1)

Tempera, on poplar panel, 12 x 8½ in. (30.5 x 21.6 cm.). Painted about 1350 – 60.

COLLECTIONS: Leighton; Benson; Duveen; Frick (1927).

In contrast to contemporary representations of this subject in Northern Europe, Barna's painting emphasizes the sorrow of Christ rather than His physical suffering. At lower left appears the diminutive kneeling figure of the presumed donor, an unidentified Dominican monk. The attribution and dating of the panel are based on its close resemblance to Barna's fresco of the *Way to Calvary* at San Gimignano.

LAZZARO BASTIANI   d. 1512

Bastiani was born in Venice and achieved considerable promi-nence there. His rather conservative style is related to that of the Vivarini and to the art of Jacopo and Gentile Bellini. According to tradition he was the teacher of Vittore Carpaccio.

Adoration of the Magi   (35.1.130)

> Tempera, on poplar panel, 20½ x 11 in. (52 x 28 cm.). Painted probably in the 1470s.
> COLLECTIONS: Abdy; Morgan; Frick (1935).

The subject of the Adoration of the Magi gave artists the op-portunity to paint sumptuous fabrics and jewels and to include exotic elements. The Frick panel employs in the background the old device of continuous narrative, weaving through the landscape various events of the Magi's journey. Attributed by some authorities to Bartolomeo Vivarini, the panel seems closer to the early works of Bastiani.

GENTILE BELLINI   c. 1429 – 1507

Gentile and his brother Giovanni were trained in the studio of their father, Jacopo Bellini. In 1474 Gentile was appointed painter to the Republic of Venice, and in this post he executed portraits and depicted Venetian pageants and ceremonies. He was in Constantinople at the court of Sultan Mohammed II in 1479 – 80.

Doge Giovanni Mocenigo   (26.1.2)

Tempera, on poplar panel, 25½ x 18¾ in. (64.8 x 47.6 cm.). Painted probably between 1478 and 1485.

COLLECTIONS: Beckford; Stothert; Langton Douglas; Frick (1926).

Giovanni Mocenigo (1408 – 85) held various civil and military posts in Venice and its territories before being elected Doge in 1478. Although a late inscription on this panel (now painted over) identified the subject as the Doge Andrea Vendramin, it seems virtually certain that the painting actually represents Mocenigo, whose features are recorded in several portraits preserved in Venice. The warm coloring and strong modeling of the portrait may reflect the influence of the artist's brother Giovanni.

4

GIOVANNI BELLINI c. 1430–1516

Giovanni Bellini began his training in the workshop of his father, Jacopo. In 1479 he succeeded his brother Gentile as painter to the Republic of Venice, and thereafter he was constantly employed by the State, as well as by Venetian churches and private patrons. He was one of the first Italian artists to master the oil technique of the Northern European painters.

St. Francis in Ecstasy (15.1.3)

Tempera and oil, on poplar panel, 49 x 55⅞ in. (124.4 x 141.9 cm.). Signed: IOANNES BELLINUS. Painted about 1480.

COLLECTIONS: Michiel; Contarini; Palazzo Corner, Venice (?); Buchanan; Murray; Dingwall; Holloway; Driver; Colnaghi and Obach; Knoedler; Frick (1915).

St. Francis of Assisi (1181/82–1226), founder of the Franciscan order, is believed to have received the Stigmata – the wounds of Christ's Crucifixion – in 1224 during a retreat on Mount Alvernia. It is probably this event that Bellini has represented here, substituting for the traditional Seraph with the Crucified Christ a more naturalistic yet transcendental imagery of rays of light from upper left flooding the foreground. In the spirit of early Franciscan literature, the artist has made eloquently predominant the landscape with its animal life and varied details.

GERARD TER BORCH 1617–1681

Ter Borch was trained in Zwolle, his birthplace, and later in Haarlem, where he painted the first of the genre scenes and portraits which were to make him famous. His extensive European travels probably brought him to Spain, where he may have studied and been influenced by the work of Velázquez.

Portrait of a Young Lady (03.1.113)

Oil, on canvas, 21⅛ x 16 in. (53.7 x 40.6 cm.). Painted about 1665 – 70.

COLLECTIONS: Thiem; Knoedler; Frick (1903).

Small-scale portraits such as this were extremely popular in Holland during the second half of the seventeenth century. Characteristic of ter Borch's manner are the elegant proportions of the figure and the skillful depiction of light playing over rich fabrics. The top and bottom of the canvas have been trimmed, indicating that the figure probably was originally full-length.

FRANÇOIS BOUCHER   1703 – 1770

Born and trained in Paris, Boucher was elected to the Academy in 1734. He subsequently won the patronage of Madame de Pompadour and was named Premier Peintre *to Louis XV. He also was associated with the Beauvais tapestry factory and later became director of the Gobelins works. Boucher's influence on the decorative arts in the mid-eighteenth century was extensive.*

Madame Boucher   (37.1.139)

Oil, on canvas, 22½ x 26⅞ in. (57.2 x 68.3 cm.). Signed and dated: *f. Boucher. 1743.*
COLLECTIONS: Bardac; David-Weill; Wildenstein; Frick (1937).

In 1743, when Boucher painted this informal portrait of his wife, Marie-Jeanne Buseau, she was twenty-seven and the mother of three children. She often posed for her husband, and in later life she learned to make miniature reproductions of his paintings and to produce etchings after his drawings. The figurine, teapot, cups, and saucers that appear in this picture reflect Boucher's taste for the *chinoiserie* so fashionable in the mid-eighteenth century.

BOUCHER

The Arts and Sciences   (16.1.4 – 16.1.11)

Poetry and Music (16.1.4)

Astronomy and Hydraulics (16.1.5)

Comedy and Tragedy (16.1.6)

Architecture and Chemistry (16.1.7)

Fishing and Hunting (16.1.8)

Fowling and Horticulture (16.1.9)

Painting and Sculpture (16.1.10)

Singing and Dancing (16.1.11)

Oil, on canvas: Nos. 4, 5, 8, 9, 85½ x 38 in. (217.2 x 96.5 cm.);
Nos. 6, 7, 10, 11, 85½ x 30½ in. (217.2 x 77.5 cm.). Painted proba-
bly between 1750 and 1753.
COLLECTIONS: de Pompadour (?); Pembroke; Barker; Wertheimer;
Sedelmeyer; Kann; Duveen; Frick (1916).

According to tradition, Madame de Pompadour commissioned
these panels for an octagonal room in the château of Crécy, an
estate she purchased in 1746 and had redecorated extensively
over the next seven years. The infants depicted personify various of the Arts and Sciences, selected perhaps to reflect the
broad range of interests of Boucher's patroness. *Architecture*,
Painting, and *Sculpture*, for example, suggest her enthusiastic
support of the arts, while *Hydraulics* was an appropriate
subject for a château whose ingenious fountains and water-
works attracted wide admiration; *Chemistry* could well allude
to the Marquise's active interest in the Vincennes porcelain
manufactory. The artist's wit is evident in such details as the
exploding experiment in *Chemistry* and the infant peering
through the wrong end of a telescope in *Astronomy*. The panels
apparently remained at Crécy until just before the destruction
of the château in 1830.

ARCHITECTURE AND
CHEMISTRY

PAINTING AND
SCULPTURE

BOUCHER

The Four Seasons (16.1.12 – 16.1.15)

Spring (16.1.12)

Summer (16.1.13)

Autumn (16.1.14)

Winter (16.1.15)

Oil, on canvas, maximum dimensions 22½ x 28¾ in. (57.2 x 73 cm.). Nos. 12, 14, 15, signed and dated: *f. Boucher 1755*.

COLLECTIONS: de Pompadour; de Marigny; Vernier; Beaujon; Ridgway; Fischhof; Bacon; Duveen; Frick (1916).

The Four Seasons were painted for Madame de Pompadour in 1755. From their shape it would appear that they were intended as overdoors, but it is not known for which of the Marquise's residences they were commissioned. Earlier representations of the seasons usually had depicted the labors associated with the various times of year; characteristically, Boucher represented pleasant pastimes instead, in the tradition of the *fête galante* established by his great predecessor Watteau. After the death of Madame de Pompadour the canvases were inherited by her brother, the Marquis de Marigny.

SPRING

BOUCHER

Drawing (16.1.16)

Poetry (16.1.17)

Oil, on canvas, both 15¾ x 12⅞ in. (40 x 32.7 cm.). Painted about 1760.

COLLECTIONS: Hertford; Wallace; Scott; Sackville; Seligmann; Knoedler; Frick (1916).

Though companion pieces, these two canvases seem to have been painted by different artists. *Drawing*, richer and warmer in coloring, may be by Boucher himself; *Poetry* probably was executed by an assistant. Various other allegories of the arts enacted by infants were painted by Boucher and his studio.

FRANÇOIS BOUCHER, Workshop of

Girl with Roses (16.1.18)

Oil, on canvas, 21½ x 16¾ in. (54.6 x 42.5 cm.). Painted probably in the 1760s.

COLLECTIONS: Hertford; Wallace; Scott; Sackville; Seligmann; Knoedler; Frick (1916).

The painting, perhaps an allegorical representation of the sense of smell, is close to Boucher's late style, but its somewhat routine manner suggests that it was possibly executed by an assistant. (Not illustrated).

11

AGNOLO BRONZINO 1503–1572

*Agnolo di Cosimo di Mariano, called Bronzino, studied with
Pontormo and later executed paintings in collaboration with him.
As court painter to Duke Cosimo I de' Medici, Bronzino was the
foremost portraitist of Florence. He also painted religious and
allegorical subjects, as well as decorations for Medici festivities.*

Lodovico Capponi (15.1.19)

Oil, on poplar panel, 45⅞ x 33¾ in. (116.5 x 85.7 cm.). Painted
probably between 1550 and 1555.

COLLECTIONS: Riccardi (?); Lucien Bonaparte; de Pourtalès-
Gorgier; Seillière; Taylor; Knoedler; Dunn; Knoedler; Frick (1915).

The youthful subject has been identified as Lodovico Capponi
(b. 1533), a page in the court of Duke Cosimo I. His finger
tantalizingly conceals the image on the cameo he holds, while
only the inscription SORTE (fate or fortune) can be read — an
ingenious illustration of the conceit that fate is obscure. Lodovico is dressed, as was his custom, in black and white, his family's armorial colors.

PIETER BRUEGEL THE ELDER
Active 1551 – 1569

The date and place of Bruegel's birth are uncertain. He entered the Antwerp painters' guild in 1551 and worked under the engraver Hieronymus Cock, for whom he supplied designs in the style of Bosch. A little later he traveled to Italy. By 1555 he was again working in Antwerp, and in 1563 he settled in Brussels. His landscapes and genre scenes had a powerful and lasting influence in the Netherlands.

The Three Soldiers   (65.1.163)

Oil, on oak panel, 8 x 7 in. (20.3 x 17.8 cm.). Signed and dated: BRUEGEL M.D[L?]XVIII.

COLLECTIONS: Charles I of England; private collection, England; Bangarth; Speelman; Agnew; Frick (1965).

This little panel represents a trio of *Landsknechte*, the mercenary soldiers who were a popular subject for printmakers in the sixteenth century. Bruegel may have painted it as a model for an engraving which was never executed, or he may have intended it simply as a cabinet piece. Quite lacking the lusty realism characteristic of the artist's genre scenes, this painting, along with a small number of other *grisailles*, perhaps reflects in its attenuated and elegant figures the influence of contemporary Italian painters.

13

HENDRIK VAN DER BURGH, Attributed to
Active 1649 – After 1669

The earliest secure record of van der Burgh is his entry as a foreigner into the painters' guild at Delft in 1649. Later he worked in Leyden and Amsterdam, chiefly painting interior genre scenes. He was strongly influenced by Pieter de Hoogh.

Drinkers Before the Fireplace   (18.1.78)

Oil, on canvas, 30½ x 26⅛ in. (77.5 x 66.3 cm.). Painted perhaps in the 1660s.

COLLECTIONS: Albrechts; Nijman; Winter; Wellesley; Napier; Goupil; Gibbs; Fischof; Frick (1918).

Both Pieter de Hoogh, to whom this canvas was long attributed, and Hendrik van der Burgh specialized in the depiction of intimate and quiet domestic scenes. However, the figures in the Frick painting and certain details such as the erratic perspective of the floor are more typical of van der Burgh's work, and the likelihood is that he was its author.

JAN VAN DE CAPPELLE, Follower of

Jan van de Cappelle (c. 1624 – 79) was born in Amsterdam, where he painted seascapes and winter landscapes from about 1645 to the mid-1660s. His calm sea and river scenes inspired a number of imitators.

A View of the River Maas
Before Rotterdam   (06.1.20)

Oil, on oak panel, 36½ x 61 in. (92.7 x 154.9 cm.).
COLLECTIONS: Lee-Mainwaring; Massey-Mainwaring; Knoedler; Frick (1906).

Among the identifiable landmarks in this scene of Rotterdam is the St. Laurenskerk, in the center distance, as it appeared after its wooden steeple was removed in 1645. The painting resembles in a general way the stately compositions of becalmed vessels that were a specialty of van de Cappelle, but many elements not characteristic of this artist suggest that it was painted by a follower, perhaps Hendrik de Meyer (c. 1620 – after 1683) or Jacob de Gruyter (active 1663 – 81).

EUGÈNE CARRIÈRE   1849 – 1906

Carrière received his first artistic training in Strasbourg but later moved to Paris, where he studied at the École des Beaux-Arts and subsequently under Cabanel. With Rodin, Puvis de Chavannes, and others, Carrière founded in 1890 the Société Nationale des Beaux-Arts, where he exhibited regularly.

Motherhood   (16.1.21)

Oil, on canvas, 22 x 18¼ in. (55.8 x 46.3 cm.). Signed: *Eugène Carrière*. Painted probably in the 1880s.

COLLECTIONS: Frick (1916).

Carrière's friends and family often modeled for his many paintings of mothers and their children. His wife, Sophie Desmousseaux, and one of his several children are portrayed in this canvas. The vaporous browns and grays, typical of most of Carrière's paintings, evoke the poetic imagery of the contemporary Symbolists as well as the sculptural style of Rodin.

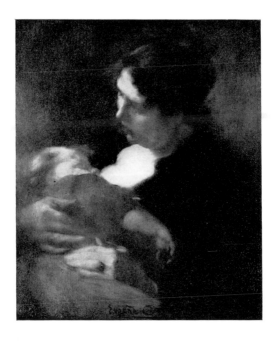

ANDREA DEL CASTAGNO, Attributed to
Before 1420 – 1457

Andrea di Bartolo di Simone was called Castagno after his birth-
place, a village in Tuscany. He worked primarily in Florence,
though his earliest dated work is the frescoed ceiling of 1442 in
S. Zaccaria, Venice. His advanced style is due in part to the in-
fluence of Masaccio. Between 1451 and 1453 he worked in col-
laboration with Domenico Veneziano and Piero della Francesca.

The Resurrection   (39.1.143)

Tempera, on poplar panel, 11¼ x 13¼ in. (28.5 x 33.7 cm.).
COLLECTIONS: Funghini (?); Fairfax Murray (?); Constantini (?);
Weisbach; Duveen; Frick (1939).

The austere dignity of the scene, with its simple composition,
gives this small panel an exceptional monumentality. In pre-
senting Christ as hovering in a *mandorla* above His tomb, the
artist follows a Florentine tradition of fusing the events of the
Resurrection and the Ascension. The painting is thought to be
one of a series of predella panels executed perhaps by Castagno but possibly by a follower for a now-lost altarpiece.

JEAN-BAPTISTE-SIMÉON CHARDIN
1699 – 1779

Chardin, the son of a cabinetmaker, was born and trained in Paris. His official recognition began in 1728 with his admission to the Academy as a genre painter. Subsequently, Louis XV awarded him commissions, a pension, and an apartment in the Louvre. Chardin's still-life paintings and scenes of middle-class domestic life were highly esteemed both within France and abroad.

Still Life with Plums   (45.1.152)

Oil, on canvas, 17¾ x 19¾ in. (45.1 x 50.2 cm.). Signed: *chardin.*
Painted probably in the late 1750s.
COLLECTIONS: Pillet; Michel-Lévy; Wildenstein; David-Weill; Wildenstein; Frick (1945).

Speaking of such typical still lifes by Chardin, with their commonplace fruits and vegetables arranged in simple pyramidal designs, Denis Diderot praised the "magic" of the artist's realism as well as his subtle color harmonies. The Cubist painters of the early twentieth century admired the bold simplicity of Chardin's compositions.

CHARDIN

Lady with a Bird-Organ (26.1.22)

Oil, on canvas, 20 x 17 in. (50.8 x 43.2 cm.). Painted in 1751 (?).
COLLECTIONS: Louis XV; de Marigny; de Tolozan; de Ladan; Didot; Vivant-Denon; Constantin; de Houdetot; Meffre; de Morny; du Tillet; Wildenstein; Frick (1926).

This painting, with its unpretentious depiction of a scene of everyday life, is a characteristic example of Chardin's figural compositions. The lady, who may in fact be the artist's wife, coaxes song from the caged canary by playing a bird-organ. The Frick canvas is one of several versions of a painting that was commissioned in 1751 by Louis XV.

CLAUDE LORRAIN   1600 – 1682

As a youth, Claude Gellée (called Lorrain after his birthplace in the French province of Lorraine) went to Rome, where he spent most of his life. His early work was chiefly in fresco, of which little remains, but his fame was based on his landscape canvases. While his patrons were largely of the Italian nobility, he also enjoyed an international reputation.

The Sermon on the Mount   (60.1.162)

Oil, on canvas, 67½ x 102¼ in. (171.4 x 259.7 cm.). Painted in 1656.

COLLECTIONS: Bosquet; Meijers; Beckford; Agar-Ellis; Grosvenor; Agnew; Heinemann; Frick (1960).

Christ, surrounded by His disciples, is shown speaking to the assembled multitude from the summit of Mount Tabor (Matthew 5:1-2). The artist has compressed the geography of the Holy Land, placing on the right the Sea of Galilee, with the towns of Tiberias and Nazareth on its shores, and on the left the Dead Sea and the river Jordan. Unusual in Claude's work is the important role played by the figures in enhancing the dramatic effect of the vast landscape. The painting was executed for François Bosquet, Bishop of Montpellier.

JOHN CONSTABLE   1776 – 1837

Constable left his native Suffolk in 1799 to study at the Royal Academy. He became an associate of the Academy in 1819 but a full member only in 1829. His landscapes, which depict chiefly the Suffolk countryside, had a deep influence on his contemporaries, particularly on the French. His elaborately finished exhibition pieces were based on numerous oil sketches painted directly from nature.

The White Horse   (43.1.147)

Oil, on canvas, 51¾ x 74⅛ in. (131.4 x 188.3 cm.). Signed and dated: *John Constable, A.R.A. / London F. 1819.*

COLLECTIONS: Fisher; Constable; Morton; Burton; Archer-Burton; Hodgson; Hemming; Agnew; Morgan; Knoedler; Frick (1943).

The painting depicts a tow-horse being ferried across the river Stour at a point where the tow-path switched from one bank to the other. The canvas was purchased by Constable's friend Archdeacon Fisher, but later was bought back by the artist, who described it as "one of my happiest efforts on a large scale." When *The White Horse* was exhibited in France in 1826, the artist was voted a gold medal. There are a number of versions of the painting, including a large canvas in the Widener Collection, National Gallery, Washington.

CONSTABLE

Salisbury Cathedral from the
Bishop's Garden   (08.1.23)

Oil, on canvas, 35 x 44¼ in. (88.9 x 112.4 cm.). Signed and dated: *John Constable. f. London. 1826.*

COLLECTIONS: Mrs. Fisher (?); Mirehouse or Pike-Scrivener; Mirehouse; Agnew; Holland; Knoedler; Frick (1908).

Constable executed several paintings of the south façade of Salisbury Cathedral seen from the Bishop's garden for his intimate friends, Dr. John Fisher, Bishop of Salisbury, and the Bishop's nephew, Archdeacon John Fisher. The latter had purchased the artist's *The White Horse* (see preceding entry) in 1819. In this version, two favorite subjects of nineteenth-century painters — a medieval ecclesiastical monument and a dramatic landscape — are ingeniously united through the arrangement of spire, gables, and tree branches.

JEAN-BAPTISTE-CAMILLE COROT
1796 – 1875

*Corot was born in Paris. During a sojourn in Italy between 1825
and 1828 he became familiar with the traditions of classical
landscape painting. After his return he painted landscapes in the
Île-de-France — especially at Ville-d'Avray — and in the forest
of Fontainebleau, and in later life he traveled and painted else-
where in Europe and throughout much of France. Corot exhibited frequently in the Salons and was awarded many honors.*

The Boatman of Mortefontaine (03.1.24)

Oil, on canvas, 24 x 35⅜ in. (60.9 x 89.8 cm.). Signed: COROT.
Painted between 1865 and 1870.

COLLECTIONS: Crabbe; Clapisson; Forbes; Coats; Knoedler;
Frick (1903).

Although inspired by the park of Mortefontaine, not far from
Paris, Corot's landscape is to a large degree imaginary. The
desire to evoke an elegiac mood led him to include, for example, the Italianate *tempietto*, which does not appear in his more
realistic charcoal study for this painting (also in The Frick Collection) or in the related *Souvenir de Mortefontaine* (Louvre).

COROT

Ville-d'Avray   (98.1.27)

Oil, on canvas, 17¼ x 29¼ in. (43.8 x 74.3 cm.). Signed: COROT.
Painted about 1860.

COLLECTIONS: Monjean (?); Grimaud; Mallet; Foinard; Roux;
de Hauff; Knoedler; Frick (1898).

The large house at the center of this painting is probably the
one which Corot owned at Ville-d'Avray, a village outside
Paris. The village and its pond recur frequently in Corot's
landscapes.

The Lake   (06.1.25)

Oil, on canvas, 52⅜ x 62 in. (133 x 157.5 cm.). Signed: COROT.
Painted in 1861.

COLLECTIONS: de Bériot; Gavet; Brun; de Fressinet de Bellanger;
Young; Knoedler; Frick (1906).

Corot exhibited *The Lake* in the Salon of 1861. Although some
contemporary critics were beginning to find such examples of
the artist's late style repetitive — Thoré, for example, said of it,
"One is not sure where one is and one has no idea where one is
going" — others praised the painting's "ravishing landscape"
and "Elysian mood." The somber, nearly monochromatic
coloring of *The Lake* and its grand scale distinguish this work
from the other landscapes by Corot in The Frick Collection.

The Pond   (99.1.26)

Oil, on canvas, 19¼ x 29 in. (48.8 x 73.6 cm.). Signed: COROT.
Painted 1868–70.

COLLECTIONS: Tempelaere; Salvator; Knoedler; Frick (1899).

The landscape is composed of motifs also found in The Frick
Collection's other Corot landscapes of the same period, and is
painted with a similar feathery touch and silver tonality.

FRANCIS COTES   1726–1770

Cotes, who was born in London, was a portraitist known chiefly for his pastels, though he also worked in oils. He was trained by Knapton but obviously knew the work of such contemporary pastelists as Rosalba Carriera, Liotard, and Latour. In 1768 he was one of the founding members of the Royal Academy.

Francis Vernon   (15.1.137)

Pastel, on paper affixed to canvas, 24 x 17⅞ in. (61 x 45.4 cm.).
Signed and dated: *FCotes pxt*: / *1757*.
COLLECTIONS: Dashwood; Grenfell; Agnew; Knoedler; Frick (1915).

This portrait of Master Francis Vernon was executed when the sitter was five years of age. The boy died only three years later. Though pastel portraiture was more popular on the Continent, Cotes achieved considerable success with the medium in England.

AELBERT CUYP   1620 – 1691

Cuyp was born in Dordrecht and spent his life there. His first works reflect the style of his father, Jacob Gerritz. Cuyp, and of the landscapist Jan van Goyen. In the 1640s, under the influence of the Italianized landscapes of Jan Both and others, he developed the luminous style which characterizes his best-known works. He painted landscapes and occasional portraits until the mid-1660s, when he appears to have ceased working.

Cows and Herdsman by a River   (02.1.28)

Oil, on oak panel, 19¾ x 29¼ in. (50.2 x 74.3 cm.). Signed: *A. cuyp*.
Painted probably in the 1650s.

COLLECTIONS: Hope; Clinton-Hope; Colnaghi and Wertheimer; Knoedler; Frick (1902).

The ruins in the background of this scene may be those of Merwede Castle, located a mile to the east of Dordrecht. Cuyp is celebrated for landscapes such as this which bring together realistic topography and an idealized Arcadian vision.

CUYP

Dordrecht: Sunrise (05.1.29)

Oil, on canvas, 40⅛ x 63⅜ in. (102 x 161 cm.). Signed: *A. cuyp*.
Painted about 1650.
COLLECTIONS: Greatheed; Percy; Knoedler; Frick (1905).

This landscape, with its golden expanse of sky and water, is one
of the artist's most ambitious attempts to render light and atmosphere. The painting may ultimately reflect the influence of
Claude Lorrain, whose landscapes impressed many of Cuyp's
countrymen and influenced their styles. Cuyp depicts Dordrecht
as seen from the north, looking across the river Merwede.
Notable among the recognizable landmarks is the Groote
Kerk, the church that appears on the horizon to the left of the
large ship in the foreground.

CUYP

River Scene
(09.1.30)

Oil, on oak panel, 23⅛ x 29⅛ in. (58.7 x 74 cm.). Signed: *A. cuyp.*
COLLECTIONS: Carlisle; Knoedler; Frick (1909).

Paintings of shipping on the inland waterways around Dordrecht were among Cuyp's specialties and permitted him to exploit intricate effects of light, such as those seen on the sails in this panel. Large ferries of the type depicted in the right foreground were among the commonest means of public transportation in the seventeenth-century Netherlands.

CHARLES-FRANÇOIS DAUBIGNY
1817 – 1878

Daubigny, the son of a Parisian painter, studied with Delaroche. He achieved his first great success in 1853, when Napoleon III bought his Salon entry. Influenced by the Barbizon painters to work directly from nature, he found many motifs for his landscapes while traveling in the countryside around Paris and during his frequent trips through Brittany, Normandy, and Picardy.

The Washerwomen   (96.1.32)

> Oil, on canvas, 20⅞ x 31½ in. (53 x 80 cm.). Signed: *Daubigny*. Painted probably between 1870 and 1874.
>
> COLLECTIONS: Sellar; Sourigne; Tavernier; Garnier; Knoedler; Frick (1896).

The Washerwomen is the earliest acquisition by Mr. Frick that still remains in the Collection. The influence of Impressionist painters is apparent here in the sketchy brushwork of the landscape.

DAUBIGNY

Dieppe (04.1.31)

Oil, on canvas, 26⅜ x 39¾ in. (67 x 101 cm.). Signed and dated:
Daubigny 1877.

COLLECTIONS: Brame (?); Cochrane; Jefferson; Cottier; Frick
(1904).

Whereas Turner's *The Harbor of Dieppe*, painted half a century
earlier and now also in The Frick Collection, recorded the
colorful, picturesque bustle of the great port, Daubigny chose
instead to depict the more somber industrial side of the city.
The painting was completed in 1877 on the basis of studies
Daubigny made at Dieppe during the previous summer. In
contrast to the execution of *The Washerwomen* (see preceding
entry), the broad, vigorous application of paint in this canvas
is typical of Daubigny's later work and suggests affinities with
the post-Impressionists.

GERARD DAVID   Active 1484 – 1523

David was born at Oudewater, near Gouda. By 1484 he was in Bruges, where he eventually succeeded Memling as chief painter of the city. He was in Antwerp in 1515 and later returned to Bruges, where he remained until his death.

The Deposition   (15.1.33)

Oil, on canvas, 56⅛ x 44¼ in. (142.5 x 112.4 cm.). Painted about 1510 – 15.

COLLECTIONS: Nieuwenhuys; Dutch Royal Collection; de Vries; Dingwall; Holloway; Driver; Colnaghi and Obach; Knoedler; Frick (1915).

The tragic dignity of the mourning figures and the austere simplicity of this composition greatly impressed David's contemporaries, and *The Deposition* and motifs from it were widely copied. This is one of the earliest examples of a Northern European painting executed in oil — rather than tempera — on canvas. It is also one of the first in which the visual qualities of the oil medium are fully exploited, most notably in the subtle ranges of the cold but vibrant tones and in the finely rendered detail of the extensive landscape.

JACQUES-LOUIS DAVID 1748–1825

Born in Paris, David won the Prix de Rome in 1774 and the following year began a five-year sojourn in Italy. An enthusiastic supporter of the French Revolution and subsequently of Napoleon, David was for a time a virtual dictator of the arts. But in 1815, after Napoleon's downfall, the artist was exiled. He retired to Brussels, where he died ten years later.

Comtesse Daru

(37.1.140)

Oil, on canvas, 32⅛ x 25⅝ in. (81.6 x 65.2 cm.). Signed and dated: *L. David / 1820.*

COLLECTIONS: Daru; David-Weill; Wildenstein; Frick (1937).

In 1802 Alexandrine-Thérèse Nardot (d. 1815) married Comte Daru, who held various high offices under Napoleon. David painted her portrait secretly in order to present it as a gift to the Count, who had assisted him in collecting payment for *Le Sacre*, David's painting of the coronation of Napoleon and Josephine. Daru's cousin, the writer Stendhal, recorded that David signed the finished work at four o'clock on March 14, 1810. The portrait is a good example of David's late style.

CÉSARINE-HENRIETTE-FLORE
DAVIN-MIRVAULT 1773–1844

Madame Davin-Mirvault, who was born in Paris, was a pupil of
David. She exhibited paintings, mostly portraits, in the Salons,
and won medals as well as a certain critical acclaim. During the
Restoration she maintained a successful school for ladies, spe-
cializing in the teaching of miniature painting.

Antonio Bartolomeo Bruni (52.1.160)

Oil, on canvas, 50⅞ x 37¾ in. (129.2 x 95.9 cm.). Painted probably
in 1804.

COLLECTIONS: Bruni; Zucconi; Bersezio; Knoedler; Frick (1952).

Composer, musician, and conductor, Bruni (1751 – 1821) was
born in Piedmont but spent much of his life in Paris. During
the Revolution he was an associate of David, to whom the
Frick portrait once was attributed. Madame Davin-Mirvault
also knew Bruni, for he occasionally performed at receptions
in her house. The direct, lively personality preserved in this
portrait, which was exhibited in the Salon of 1804, is similar
to that of David's portrait of the Comtesse Daru, also in The
Frick Collection.

HILAIRE-GERMAIN-EDGAR DEGAS
1834 – 1917

Degas, who was born in Paris, studied at the École des Beaux-Arts. After a trip to Italy in 1856 he settled in Paris, where he exhibited at the Salons from 1865 to 1870. In 1872 he visited New Orleans, and later in life he made trips on the Continent, to England, and to North Africa. He exhibited for eight years with the Impressionists, but his interests and style diverged somewhat from theirs. His varied subjects — motifs drawn largely from urban life — included ballet dancers, women bathing, and race horses.

The Rehearsal   (14.1.34)

Oil, on canvas, 18¾ x 24 in. (47.6 x 60.9 cm.). Signed: *Degas*.
Painted probably in 1878 or early 1879.
COLLECTIONS: Rouart; Knoedler; Frick (1914).

In his choice of ballet subjects, Degas largely avoided dramatic moments of stage performance in favor of rehearsal scenes, as in this painting. The dancers' conventionalized movements give them a somewhat dehumanized air — a quality Degas captured as well in his depictions of bathers. This canvas probably was shown at the fourth exhibition of the Impressionists in 1879.

FRANÇOIS-HUBERT DROUAIS 1727–1775

Of Norman extraction, Drouais spent all his life in and around Paris. In 1757 he executed his first royal commission, and the following year he was received as full member in the Academy. Succeeding Latour and Nattier, Drouais became the most prominent French portraitist of the mid-eighteenth century, painting courtiers, foreign aristocrats, writers, and other artists.

The Comte and Chevalier de Choiseul as Savoyards
(66.1.164)

> Oil, on canvas, 54⅞ x 42 in. (139.4 x 106.7 cm.). Signed and dated: *Drouais le fils | 1758.*
> COLLECTIONS: de Choiseul; Digeon; de Rothschild; Wildenstein; Frick (1966).

Marie-Gabriel-Florent-Auguste, Comte de Choiseul-Beaupré (1752–1817), stands beside his younger brother, Michel-Félix-Victor, Chevalier de Choiseul-Daillecourt (1754–1815). Drouais has disguised his subjects as Savoyards, the gypsy-like migrants from Savoy who wandered over France doing menial work and performing in street fairs. Since the Savoyards were considered models of filial devotion because of their attachment to their homeland and families, the artist seems to have used this disguise with a specific symbolic intention.

DUCCIO DI BUONINSEGNA c. 1255–1319

Although Duccio was the leading Sienese master of his time, little is known of his life. He is first mentioned in a document of 1278, and in 1285 he received the commission for a painting of the Madonna assumed to be the Rucellai Madonna now in the Uffizi. His greatest work is the Maestà, an altarpiece painted for the Duomo of Siena.

The Temptation of Christ
on the Mountain   (27.1.35)

Tempera, on poplar panel, 17 x 18⅛ in. (43.2 x 46 cm.). Painted 1308–11.

COLLECTIONS: Duomo of Siena; Dini (?); Fairfax Murray (?); Benson; Duveen; Frick (1927).

Christ is seen rejecting the devil, who offers Him "all the kingdoms of the world" if He will worship him (Matthew 4:8-11). Duccio retains medieval conventions in representing the figures as very large and the rejected kingdoms as very small, thus suggesting symbolically a scale of relative values rather than one of naturalistic proportions. The panel is one of a series of scenes from the life of Christ painted on the reverse of Duccio's *Maestà*, commissioned in 1308 and completed in 1311.

JULES DUPRÉ   1811–1889

Dupré, who was born in Nantes, was influenced by the Dutch landscapists and by Constable. He exhibited occasionally in the Salons and was associated with painters of the Barbizon group, including Rousseau, Troyon, and Daubigny.

The River   (97.1.36)

Oil, on canvas, 17 x 23 in. (43.2 x 58.4 cm.).
COLLECTIONS: Gavet; Laurent-Richard; de Rothschild; Knoedler; Frick (1897).

The influence of Constable's oil sketches on Dupré's landscapes is very apparent in this work, where short, broken brushstrokes are skillfully used in the depiction of evanescent effects of light and atmosphere. The canvas was shown at the Exposition Universelle in Paris in 1867.

SIR ANTHONY VAN DYCK 1599–1641

Van Dyck was born in Antwerp, where he worked under Hendrik van Balen and Rubens. He visited London in 1620 and traveled and worked in Italy from 1621 until 1627, when he returned to Antwerp. From 1632 until his death he was active chiefly in England, where he was knighted by Charles I and became the leading portrait painter of the court and aristocracy.

James, Seventh Earl of Derby, His Lady and Child (13.1.40)

Oil, on canvas, 97 x 84⅛ in. (246.4 x 213.7 cm.). Painted between 1632 and 1641.

COLLECTIONS: Clarendon; Knoedler; Frick (1913).

This work, typical of the large group portraits the artist painted during his last English period, represents James Stanley, Lord Strange, seventh Earl of Derby, with his wife Charlotte de la Trémoille and one of their daughters. The Earl was a writer of history and of devotional books, as well as a Royalist commander during the Civil War. He was captured and executed by Commonwealth forces in 1651. During the war his wife became famous for her spirited defense of Latham House, the Derbys' country seat.

VAN DYCK

Frans Snyders (09.1.39)

Oil, on canvas, 56⅛ x 41½ in. (142.5 x 105.4 cm.). Painted about 1620.

COLLECTIONS: de Nossé; d'Orléans; Slade; Carlisle; Knoedler; Frick (1909).

Snyders (1579–1657) was a celebrated painter of still lifes, animals, and hunting scenes, and often assisted Rubens in these capacities. He was an intimate friend of Van Dyck, who also etched a portrait of Snyders for his *Icones centum*, published in 1645. The Frick painting and its companion portrait of Snyders' wife Margareta (see following entry) were executed in Antwerp, and are much closer to Rubens' style than the works of Van Dyck's later English period.

VAN DYCK

Margareta Snyders (09.1.42)

>Oil, on canvas, 51½ x 39⅛ in. (130.7 x 99.3 cm.). Painted about 1620.
>
>COLLECTIONS: de Nossé; d'Orléans; Slade; Warwick; Knoedler; Frick (1909).

Margareta de Vos was a sister of the painters Cornelis and Paul de Vos and the wife of Frans Snyders, whom she married in 1611. This portrait is a companion to Van Dyck's portrait of her husband (see preceding entry), and the still-life detail of flowers in the upper left may be a reference to Snyders' specialty in that field of painting.

VAN DYCK

Paola Adorno, Marchesa di
Brignole Sale (14.1.43)

Oil, on canvas, 90⅞ x 61⅝ in. (230.8 x 156.5 cm.). Painted between 1622 and 1627.

COLLECTIONS: Aberdeen; Abercorn; Frick (1914).

Paola, the daughter of Giambattista Adorno, Senator and Governor of Genoa, married Anton Giulio Brignole, a poet, writer, and political figure, who entered the priesthood after her death in 1648. Van Dyck painted her likeness more than once during his sojourn in Genoa. The elegantly elongated proportions he used in portraits such as this became a hallmark of his later style.

VAN DYCK

Marchesa Giovanna Cattaneo (07.1.41)

Oil, on canvas, 40⅜ x 34 in. (102.6 x 86.4 cm.). Painted between 1622 and 1627.

COLLECTIONS: Cattaneo; Knoedler; Frick (1907).

Giovanna Battista Cattaneo, traditionally identified as the subject of this portrait, was the daughter of the Marchese Giovanni Battista Cattaneo of Genoa. The heavy gold chain (*catena*) she so conspicuously displays is probably a play on the family name. Judging from the abrupt termination of the figure, it would seem that the portrait has been cut down from a larger format.

Ottaviano Canevari (05.1.38)

Oil, on canvas, 51¼ x 39 in. (130.2 x 99.1 cm.). Painted probably in 1627.

COLLECTIONS: Lomellini (?); Cattaneo; Knoedler; Frick (1905).

Ottaviano Canevari was a Genoese magistrate and Senator, and brother of the renowned Demetrio Canevari, a physician, writer, and bibliophile who once was thought to be the subject of this portrait. When Demetrio died in 1625 he left in trust a vast library and named Ottaviano literary executor, which may explain why Van Dyck included in the painting volumes by Hippocrates and Aristotle.

43

VAN DYCK

Anne, Countess of Clanbrassil (17.1.37)

Oil, on canvas, 83½ x 50¼ in. (212.1 x 127.6 cm.). Painted probably in 1636.

COLLECTIONS: Buckingham(?); Torrington; Denbigh; Frick (1917).

Lady Anne Carey (d. 1689), daughter of the second Earl of Monmouth, was married in 1635 to James Hamilton, second Viscount Claneboye, later Earl of Clanbrassil. An old source describes Lady Anne as "very handsome, and witty . . . a woman extraordinary in knowledge, virtue, and piety." Such characteristic portraits by Van Dyck, with their gracefully attenuated figures posed in natural settings, had a marked influence in the eighteenth century on Reynolds, Gainsborough, and even Goya.

VAN DYCK

Sir John Suckling (18.1.44)

Oil, on canvas, 85¼ x 51¼ in. (216.5 x 130.2 cm.). Painted between 1632 and 1641.

COLLECTIONS: Southcott; Lee; Frick (1918).

In his own day, Suckling (1609–42) was famous not only as a lyric poet, but also as a flamboyant figure at court and a military adventurer under Charles I and Gustavus Adolphus of Sweden. Implicated in a political plot, he fled to Paris, where he later committed suicide. In this portrait Suckling holds a volume of Shakespeare opened to *Hamlet*, evidently in tribute to the writer who strongly influenced his own work and to the play from which he often borrowed language and ideas.

JAN VAN EYCK   Active 1422–1441

Completed by an Assistant, Perhaps Petrus Christus (Active 1441 – 1472/73)

Van Eyck, born near Maastricht, worked in The Hague for the Count of Holland, and in 1425 was made court painter to the Duke of Burgundy. Most of his datable paintings were executed in Bruges in the 1430s.

Virgin and Child, with Saints and Donor   (54.1.161)

Oil, on panel, 18⅝ x 24⅛ in. (47.3 x 61.3 cm.). Painted probably in the early 1440s.

COLLECTIONS: de Rothschild; Knoedler; Frick (1954).

The Virgin is flanked at the left by St. Barbara and at the right by St. Elizabeth of Hungary. Kneeling in the foreground is Jan Vos, Prior of the Carthusian Charterhouse of Genadedal, near Bruges, who commissioned the work. Most modern scholars consider this one of the artist's last paintings, ordered in Bruges in 1441 and begun by van Eyck but completed in his shop. The assistant involved may have been Petrus Christus, but it is not possible to rule out the existence of another collaborator, as yet unidentified.

JEAN-HONORÉ FRAGONARD   1732–1806

Born in Grasse, Fragonard studied briefly with Chardin and then with Boucher. In 1752 he won the Prix de Rome, and from 1756 to 1761 he worked at the French Academy in Rome. After his return to Paris he became one of the favorite artists of Louis XV and his court, much in demand for his blithe pastoral romantic subjects, landscapes, and decorative paintings. Sympathetic to the Revolution and a friend of Jacques-Louis David, he held various appointments after 1790 until, under the Directory, he was dismissed from all public offices. He died in poverty.

The Progress of Love   (15.1.45 – 15.1.55)

> COLLECTIONS: du Barry (?); Maubert; Malvilan; Wertheimer; Agnew; Morgan; Duveen; Frick (1915).

The first four panels of *The Progress of Love* — *The Pursuit*, *The Meeting*, *Love Letters*, and *The Lover Crowned* — were commissioned by Madame du Barry for a new dining pavilion in the garden of her château at Louveciennes. Begun probably in 1771, they were seen at Louveciennes in 1772 and described in the press as not yet finished, but eventually they were rejected, possibly because their rococo style seemed old-fashioned in a building designed in the current classicizing manner. Joseph-Marie Vien provided suitable replacements in a neo-classical style, and Fragonard retained his paintings until, in 1790, he returned to his native Grasse. There he installed the Louveciennes panels in the main salon of his cousin Maubert's house and executed two more large panels, four overdoor compositions, and the four *Hollyhocks* panels to complete the decoration. The entire group is exhibited at The Frick Collection except for three of the *Hollyhocks* panels. Comparison with preparatory drawings and oil sketches for the paintings demonstrates that Fragonard made crucial compositional changes during their execution. The Frick canvases, with their grand scale and elaborate compositions, are major examples of Fragonard's art, and indeed rank among the outstanding achievements of French decorative painting of the eighteenth century.

THE PURSUIT

FRAGONARD

The Progress of Love

The Pursuit (15.1.45)

125⅛ x 84⅞ in. (317.8 x 215.5 cm.).

The Meeting (15.1.46)

125 x 96 in. (317.5 x 243.8 cm.).

Love Letters (15.1.47)

124⅞ x 85⅜ in. (317.1 x 216.8 cm.).

The Lover Crowned (15.1.48)

125⅛ x 95¾ in. (317.8 x 243.2 cm.).

NOS. 45-48. Oil on canvas. Signed: *fragonard*. Painted probably between 1771 and 1773.

Reverie (15.1.49)

125⅛ x 77⅝ in. (317.8 x 197.1 cm.).

Love Triumphant (15.1.50)

125 x 56½ in. (317.5 x 143.5 cm.).

Love the Avenger (15.1.51)

59⅜ x 50⅜ in. (150.8 x 127.9 cm.).

Love Pursuing a Dove (15.1.52)

59⅝ x 47¾ in. (151.4 x 121.2 cm.).

Love the Jester (15.1.53)

59⅜ x 50⅜ in. (150.8 x 127.9 cm.).

Love the Sentinel (15.1.54)

57⅝ x 47½ in. (146.3 x 120.6 cm.).

Hollyhocks (15.1.55 A-D)

Nos. 55A, 55C, 125¼ x 25 in. (318.2 x 63.5 cm.); Nos. 55B, 55D, 125½ x 16⅜ in. (318.8 x 41.6 cm.).

NOS. 49-55. Oil on canvas. Painted probably 1790–91.

THE
MEETING

LOVE
LETTERS

THE
LOVER
CROWNED

REVERIE

51

FRENCH, Probably Burgundian   About 1390 – 1400

Virgin and Child   (27.1.57)

Oil and tempera, on panel: 8⅝ x 5⅝ in. (21.9 x 14.3 cm.); with frame, 12⅛ x 9¼ in. (30.8 x 23.5 cm.).

COLLECTIONS: Private collection, Tours; Durlacher; Frick (1927).

The national origin of this *Virgin and Child* is uncertain, as are the origins of so many late Gothic paintings. The artist appears to have been familiar with Italian painting of the period, as well as with the art of France and the Netherlands. The tender sentiment, rich coloring, and decorative patterning of the panel appear in works from many European centers, but the style comes closest to Burgundian painting of the late fourteenth century. The panel and its carved frame are made from a single piece of wood.

FRENCH, Probably South of France   Fifteenth Century

Pietà with Donor   (07.1.56)

Tempera or mixed technique, on panel, 15⅝ x 22 in. (39.7 x 55.8 cm.).

COLLECTIONS: Convent in Catalonia (?); Renouvier; d'Albenas; Gross; Shirleys; Frick (1907).

The Pietà, or representation of the Virgin supporting the dead Christ — an image poignantly recalling the Virgin holding the Christ Child — first appears in Germanic art of the fourteenth century. Here it is presented in an imaginary landscape which includes in the background a Gothic town probably intended to represent Jerusalem. This panel, once attributed to Antonello da Messina, now is believed to have been painted in Savoy or possibly in eastern Provence around the middle or during the second half of the fifteenth century. It is a copy, slightly enlarged and with compositional variations, of another *Pietà*, without a donor figure, now in the collection of Miss Helen C. Frick. The latter panel has been ascribed to Konrad Witz or a follower.

53

THOMAS GAINSBOROUGH   1727–1788

Gainsborough, who was born in Sudbury, Suffolk, went to London in 1740. He worked with the French engraver Hubert Gravelot and probably with the painter Francis Hayman. He painted at Ipswich between 1752 and 1759, then moved to Bath, where he remained until his return to London in 1774. Gainsborough was a founding member of the Royal Academy. Though best known for his portraits, he also painted landscapes.

Sarah, Lady Innes   (14.1.58)

Oil, on canvas, 40 x 28⅝ in. (101.6 x 72.7 cm.). Painted about 1757.
COLLECTIONS: Innes; Fairholme; Colnaghi; Dunn; Knoedler; Frick (1914).

The sitter is traditionally identified as Sarah (d. 1770), the daughter and heiress of Thomas Hodges of Ipswich. She was the second wife of Sir William Innes, captain of the Second Light Dragoons. Painted early in Gainsborough's career, the portrait is conventional in its stiffly mannered pose, but the diaphanous textures and softly brushed, moody landscape presage the artist's mature style.

GAINSBOROUGH

Richard Paul Jodrell (46.1.154)

Oil, on canvas, 30¼ x 25⅛ in. (76.8 x 63.8 cm.). Painted about 1774.

COLLECTIONS: Jodrell; Agnew; Ruston; Agnew; Harland-Peck; Palmer; Duveen; Frick (1946).

Jodrell (1745–1831) was a barrister, classical scholar, philologist, and dramatist, and a friend of Dr. Johnson. This portrait probably was painted just before Gainsborough left Bath or shortly after he moved to London in 1774. With its technique of transparent glazes of color, the portrait possesses that quality which Gainsborough's rival Sir Joshua Reynolds singled out for praise: "the lightness of effect which is so eminent a beauty in his work."

GAINSBOROUGH

The Hon. Frances Duncombe   (11.1.61)

Oil, on canvas, 92¼ x 61⅛ in. (234.3 x 155.2 cm.). Painted about 1777.

COLLECTIONS: Bowater; Sawyer; Graves; de Rothschild; Wertheimer; Duveen; Frick (1911).

The subject was born in 1757, the only daughter by his second wife of Anthony Duncombe, Lord Feversham. Gainsborough painted a half-length portrait of Frances in 1773, as well as one of her half-sister Anne in 1778. The Frick portrait offers clear testimony to the artist's enthusiasm for Van Dyck; not only did Gainsborough share the seventeenth-century artist's taste for elegant proportions, graceful poses, and Arcadian settings, but even the costume reflects the fashions of an earlier time.

GAINSBOROUGH

Mrs. Peter William Baker (17.1.59)

Oil, on canvas, 89⅝ x 59¾ in. (227.6 x 151.8 cm.). Signed and
dated: *Thos. Gainsborough | 1781.*

COLLECTIONS: Baker; Duveen; Frick (1917).

The subject, Jane (d. 1816), daughter of James Clitherow, married Peter William Baker of Ranston, Dorset, in 1781 — the
year Gainsborough executed this portrait. The artist also
painted portraits of Mr. Baker's parents. The mannered ele-
gance of late works such as this contrasts with the brisk direct-
ness of Gainsborough's earlier portrait of *Lady Innes*. The
natural setting, lacking architectural elements such as appear
in the portrait of *The Hon. Frances Duncombe*, recalls Gainsborough's dramatic landscape paintings from the same period.

GAINSBOROUGH

Mrs. Charles Hatchett (03.1.60)

Oil, on canvas, 29¾ x 24⅝ in.
(75.5 x 62.5 cm.). Painted perhaps
in 1786. Inscribed(?): GD.
COLLECTIONS: Hatchett (?); de
Rothschild; Wertheimer; Lawrie;
Coats; Knoedler; Frick (1903).

The subject is Elizabeth Collick (d.
1837), a gifted pianist who married
Charles Hatchett, the discoverer
of the rare metal columbium and
a friend of the leading intellectuals
of his day. The Hatchetts appear
to have been closely associated with Gainsborough, who shared
their musical interests.

Grace Dalrymple Elliott (46.1.153)

Oil, on canvas, 30⅛ x 25 in. (76.5
x 63.5 cm.). Painted probably in
1782.
COLLECTIONS: Bentinck (?); Port-
land; Duveen; Frick (1946).

Grace Dalrymple (c. 1754–1823)
married Sir John Elliott in 1771,
but was divorced by him five years
later. A tall and beautiful woman,
her liaisons won her considerable
notoriety. Among her admirers
were the Prince of Wales (who may
have commissioned this portrait), Lord Cholmondeley, and
Philippe Égalité, Duc d'Orléans. She remained in Paris during
the French Revolution and later published a *Journal* of her ex-
periences.

GAINSBOROUGH

The Mall in St. James's Park (16.1.62)

Oil, on canvas, 47½ x 57⅞ in. (120.6 x 147 cm.). Painted probably in 1783.

COLLECTIONS: Elwin; Howe (or Home); Frost; Kilderbee; Bone; Neeld; Hanbury; Agnew; Duveen; Frick (1916).

St. James's Park was near Gainsborough's London residence, Schomberg House, in Pall Mall. *The Mall*, with its figure groups set in a landscape, is unusual among the artist's later works. As several contemporary writers stated, it recalls the *fêtes galantes* of Watteau. The feathery trees and rhythmic design led one observer to describe the painting as "all aflutter, like a lady's fan." The artist reportedly composed the painting partly from dolls and a model of the setting.

GENTILE DA FABRIANO c. 1370 – 1427

*Born in Fabriano, near Urbino, Gentile is first recorded in 1408
in Venice. He worked there, in Brescia, and probably in other
north Italian towns before moving to Tuscany around 1420. During the next few years he received important commissions from
churches and great families of Siena, Florence, and Orvieto, and
by 1427 he had left for Rome to paint the frescoes, now lost, in
St. John Lateran.*

Madonna and Child, with
Saints Lawrence and Julian (66.1.167)

Tempera, on panel, 35¾ x 18½ in. (90.8 x 47 cm.). Signed (on the
frame): *gentili*[*s*?] [*de*?].... Painted about 1423–25.

COLLECTIONS: Private collection, France (purchased in Italy in
1846); Frick (1966).

This small but richly painted altarpiece was designed perhaps
for some private family chapel. It must be close in date to
Gentile's best-known work, the *Adoration of the Magi*, commissioned in 1423 by the Strozzi family of Florence and now
in the Uffizi. Like the *Adoration*, this panel, with its elegantly
ornamented surface of glittering gold leaf and brilliant color,

perpetuates late Gothic traditions, most obviously in the
gentle, graceful figures of Madonna and Child. The kneeling
Saints, however, seem more advanced than work of the same
date by Gentile's contemporaries in Florence; the portrait-like heads and solidly modeled
bodies are strikingly natural
and eloquent. St. Lawrence, the
third-century martyr, is identified by the grid on which he was
burned alive. St. Julian, who
wears knightly robes and carries
a sword, built a hospital for
travelers.

FRANCISCO DE GOYA Y LUCIENTES
1746 – 1828

Born in Fuendetodos, near Saragossa, Goya studied with José Luzán and then with Francisco Bayeu, whose sister he married. He went to Italy in 1771, worked in Saragossa in 1772, and in 1774 was commissioned to become a designer for the Royal Tapestry Factory in Madrid. Appointed court painter to Charles IV in 1786, he continued in that post under Ferdinand VII. In addition to portraits, Goya painted historical, religious, and genre subjects, bitter satires, and demonological fantasies; he also was a brilliant graphic artist. In 1824, out of favor with the court, he went to France and settled in Bordeaux, where he died.

An Officer (Conde de Tepa ?)   (14.1.64)

Oil, on canvas, 24⅞ x 19¼ in. (63.2 x 48.9 cm.).
COLLECTIONS: Galdeano; Ehrich; Frick (1914).

The intense and wary young officer Goya portrayed has yet to be convincingly identified, although various gentlemen have been proposed as subjects. The most likely candidate is Don Francisco Leandro de Viana, Conde de Tepa, a nobleman active in Spanish colonial affairs.

GOYA

Don Pedro, Duque de Osuna (43.1.151)

Oil, on canvas, 44½ x 32¾ in. (113 x 83.2 cm.). Signed: *Por Goya*.
Painted probably in the 1790s.

COLLECTIONS: Osuna; Dannat (with Linden?); Agnew; Morgan;
Knoedler; Frick (1943).

Don Pedro de Alcántara Téllez-Girón y Pacheco (1755–1807),
ninth Duque de Osuna, was one of Spain's wealthiest and most
talented noblemen during the reigns of Charles III and Charles
IV. After the royal court, he was Goya's most faithful patron,
commissioning more than twenty-four works from the artist.

GOYA

The Forge   (14.1.65)

Oil, on canvas, 71½ x 49¼ in. (181.6 x 125.1 cm.). Painted about
1815–20.

COLLECTIONS: Javier Goya; Louis-Philippe of France; Taunton;
Stanley; Agnew; Colnaghi and Knoedler; Frick (1914).

The painting is executed in the rough, vigorous style of Goya's
later years, but is unconventional for the period in its monumental treatment of a contemporary industrial subject. An
earlier, closely similar, idea for this composition can be seen
in a Goya drawing of three men digging, now in the Metro-
politan Museum, New York.

GOYA

Doña María Martínez de Puga   (14.1.63)

Oil, on canvas, 31½ x 23 in. (80 x 58.4 cm.). Signed and dated:
Goya 1824.

COLLECTIONS: de Beruete y Moret; Lane; Dunn; Colnaghi and
Knoedler; Frick (1914).

The sober, almost monochromatic palette and the broad handling of paint in this work are characteristic of Goya's portraits in the last years of his life. The date, 1824, indicates that
the portrait could have been painted in Madrid shortly before
the artist went to France, or in Paris or Bordeaux later that
year. When Mr. Frick acquired the painting, the sitter was described as either Goya's landlady in Bordeaux or her daughter,
but neither identification has been substantiated.

DOMENIKOS THEOTOKOPOULOS
(EL GRECO) 1541–1614

El Greco was born in Crete and probably learned to paint there in the Byzantine manner. As a youth he went to Venice, where he reputedly studied with Titian. He was in Rome in 1570, and by 1577 he had moved to Toledo, where he settled for the rest of his life. His style was influenced not only by Titian, but also by Tintoretto and Jacopo Bassano, and later by Michelangelo.

Vincenzo Anastagi (13.1.68)

Oil, on canvas, 74 x 49⅞ in. (188 x 126.3 cm.). Signed in Greek characters. Painted about 1571–76.

COLLECTIONS: Coningham; Farrer; Labouchere; Stanley; Colnaghi and Knoedler; Frick (1913).

Anastagi (c. 1531–86) held high offices in the Order of the Knights of Malta, leading his troops to victory against the Turks in 1565 and later becoming sergeant-major of Castel Sant' Angelo in Rome. This portrait, Venetian in conception but already characteristically intense and spirited in style, was painted probably during El Greco's last years in Italy.

EL GRECO

St. Jerome (05.1.67)

Oil, on canvas, 43½ x 37½ in. (110.5 x 95.3 cm.). Signed in Greek characters. Painted about 1590–1600.

COLLECTIONS: Valladolid Cathedral (?); Pares; Bourdariat; Trotti; Knoedler; Frick (1905).

St. Jerome (c. 342–420) was widely venerated for his scholarship and ascetic piety. The open book on which his hands rest in the Frick painting probably represents the Latin Vulgate, his monumental translation of the Bible. Following an old tradition, El Greco depicts the Saint in the robes of a cardinal. This composition evidently proved popular, for El Greco and his studio produced at least four versions of it.

EL GRECO

Purification of the Temple (09.1.66)

Oil, on canvas, 16½ x 20⅝ in. (41.9 x 52.4 cm.). Painted about 1600.

COLLECTIONS: Infante Don Antonio de Borbón (?); Herreros de Tejada (?); Vest-Servet; de Beruete y Moret; Frick (1909).

The subject of Christ driving the traders and money-changers from the temple was especially popular during the Counter Reformation as an allegorical reference to the purification of the Church. El Greco and his shop made several versions of the subject, the Frick canvas being one of the later examples. The brilliant but cold hues and the explosive, angular design of the composition enhance the dramatic impact of this small painting.

JEAN-BAPTISTE GREUZE   1725 – 1805

Born in Tournus, Greuze went to Paris in the 1750s and studied at the Academy. In 1755, the year he first exhibited at the Salon, he began a year's sojourn in Italy. He was made a member of the Academy in 1769. Engravings popularized Greuze's anecdotal, often moralizing, genre scenes and brought the artist considerable wealth.

The Wool Winder   (43.1.148)

Oil, on canvas, 29⅜ x 24⅛ in. (74.6 x 61.3 cm.). Painted in 1759.
COLLECTIONS: de Bandol; La Live de Jully; Catelin; de Choiseul; de Bandeville; Desmarets; de Ségur; de Morny; de Sesto; Montaignac and Sedelmeyer; Hertford; Wallace; Wertheimer; Walter; Morgan; Knoedler; Frick (1943).

Like most of Greuze's early work, *The Wool Winder* is related to Chardin's genre pictures of the 1730s. However, Greuze's genre scenes are usually—as is the case with this picture—more whimsical and anecdotal than those of his predecessor. The painting was exhibited in the Salon of 1759.

FRANS HALS 1581/85 – 1666

Hals probably was born in Antwerp. By 1591 he had emigrated with his parents to Haarlem, where he is believed to have studied with Carel van Mander and where he joined the painters' guild in 1610. He remained in Haarlem until his death, painting chiefly portraits, including a number of important group portraits commissioned by militia officers and governors of charitable institutions.

Portrait of an Elderly Man   (10.1.69)

Oil, on canvas, 45½ x 36 in. (115.6 x 91.4 cm.). Painted about 1627–30.

COLLECTIONS: Arundell; Wertheimer; Sedelmeyer; Kann; Duveen; Frick (1910).

The technique of this portrait dating from Hals' early maturity is derived in part from Rubens. The thin, fluid handling of paint, the warm but restricted color scheme, the sitter's animated expression, and his air of confident self-assertion are typical of Hals' major works from these years.

HOBBEMA

Village with Water Mill Among Trees (11.1.74)

Oil, on canvas, 37⅛ x 51⅛ in. (94.3 x 129.8 cm.). Signed: *meynd ʳᵗ / hobbema*.

COLLECTIONS: Burlington; Knoedler; Frick (1911).

Comparison of this canvas with the preceding *Village Among Trees,* which dates from about the same period, clearly demonstrates that although Hobbema's repertory of motifs observed in nature was limited, he invested his paintings with considerable freshness and variety.

WILLIAM HOGARTH   1697 – 1764

Hogarth lived all his life in London. He learned the technique of engraving during his apprenticeship to a silver-plate engraver, and he later studied drawing with Thornhill. His fame among his contemporaries depended chiefly on the engravings he made of moral satires, which he executed first as paintings. He also painted portraits and was the author of an autobiography and a treatise on aesthetics.

Miss Mary Edwards   (14.1.75)

> Oil, on canvas, 49¾ x 37⅞ in. (126.4 x 101.3 cm.). Signed and dated: W. HOGARTH 1742.
>
> COLLECTIONS: Edwards; Noel; Knoedler; Frick (1914).

Mary Edwards (1705–43), one of the richest women of her time, was the daughter of Francis Edwards of Welham Grove, Leicestershire. She was married clandestinely to Lord Anne Hamilton, but later, apparently to protect her fortune, she had the marriage repudiated and gave her maiden name to her son. Hogarth's frank and rather informal approach to portraiture clearly suited the personality of his subject.

75

HANS HOLBEIN THE YOUNGER
1497/98 – 1543

Holbein was the son of the Augsburg painter Hans Holbein (the Elder), who probably gave him his first training. In 1514 he went to Basel, where he achieved great success. He visited England in 1526–28, and in 1532 he returned to settle there, eventually becoming court painter to Henry VIII.

Sir Thomas More   (12.1.77)

Oil, on oak panel, 29½ x 23¾ in. (74.9 x 60.3 cm.). Dated: M. D. XXVII.

COLLECTIONS: Farrer; Huth; Knoedler; Frick (1912).

More (1477/78–1535) was a lawyer, statesman, and humanist scholar, and the author of *Utopia* (1516), a treatise on the ideal state. Early in his career he attracted the attention of the young Henry VIII, who chose him for many diplomatic missions and made him privy councilor. More was elected speaker of the House of Commons and later succeeded Cardinal Wolsey as Lord Chancellor. In 1532 he resigned his office over the issue of Henry's divorce from Catherine of Aragon, and two years later he refused to subscribe to the Acts of Supremacy and Succession; for this he was sentenced to death for high treason. More was canonized in 1935.

Thomas Cromwell   (15.1.76)

Oil, on oak panel, 30⅞ x 25⅜ in. (78.4 x 64.4 cm.).

COLLECTIONS: Pope (?); Hardwicke; Caledon; Lane; Frick (1915).

Cromwell was born about 1485, the son of a Putney blacksmith. He entered Cardinal Wolsey's service in 1514 and held various high positions under Henry VIII, culminating in his appointment as Lord Great Chamberlain in 1539. He was largely responsible for the execution of Sir Thomas More. In 1540 Cromwell lost royal favor, and, accused of treason, was himself beheaded. Of the several versions of this portrait, the Frick example is considered the best and oldest, but is probably based on a lost Holbein original.

JOHN HOPPNER 1758-1810

Hoppner was born in London. He entered the Royal Academy in 1775, first exhibited there in 1780, and eventually was made full Academician. As a portraitist he enjoyed great popularity and served as portrait painter to the Prince of Wales (later George IV).

The Hon. Lucy Byng   (99.1.79)

Oil, on canvas, 30⅛ x 25 in. (76.5 x 63.5 cm.).
COLLECTIONS: Byng; Knoedler; Frick (1899).

Some uncertainty exists over the identity of the subject, who may be either Lucy Elizabeth Byng (1794–1875), daughter of Vice-Admiral George Byng, sixth Viscount Torrington, or another Lucy Elizabeth Byng, daughter of George Byng, fourth Viscount Torrington. Hoppner's feathery style did not vary sufficiently to permit a dating on stylistic evidence.

HOPPNER

The Ladies Sarah and Catherine Bligh (15.1.80)

Oil, on canvas, 51⅛ x 40⅜ in. (129.8 x 102.5 cm.). Painted about 1790.
COLLECTIONS: Darnley; Knoedler; Frick (1915).

Lady Sarah Bligh (1772–97) and her sister Lady Catherine (1774–1812) were the youngest children of John Bligh, third Earl of Darnley. The background landscape in this portrait may depict the Thames at Gravesend, as seen from the Bligh estate, Cobham Park.

JEAN-AUGUSTE-DOMINIQUE INGRES
1780 – 1867

Born in Montauban, Ingres studied with David in Paris after a precocious start at Toulouse. He won the Prix de Rome in 1801 and was in Italy from 1806 until 1824. He spent the following decade in Paris, where he received official honors and attracted many students, then returned to Rome for seven years as Director of the French Academy. His final years were spent in Paris.

Comtesse d'Haussonville   (27.1.81)

> Oil, on canvas, 51⅞ x 36¼ in. (131.8 x 92 cm.). Signed and dated:
> INGRES. / 1845.
> COLLECTIONS: d'Haussonville; Wildenstein; Frick (1927).

Louise, Princesse de Broglie (1818–82), married at the age of eighteen. Her husband was a diplomat, writer, and member of the French Academy, and she herself published a number of books, including a life of Byron. This portrait, begun in 1842, was the fruit of several false starts and of many preparatory drawings, one of which is in The Frick Collection. When finished, according to a letter written by the artist, the portrait "aroused a storm of approval."

JACQUES DE LAJOUE, Attributed to
1686/87 – 1761

The son of an architect, Lajoue was born in Paris. By 1721 he was an associate of the Academy, where he exhibited until 1753. A painter of landscapes, seascapes, interiors, and animal studies, he assisted in the decoration of many châteaux and royal palaces.

Seven Decorative Panels Mounted in a Screen
(16.1.82 A-G)

Oil, on canvas: Nos. 82A, 82C, 82E, 82G, 58⅝ x 21½ in. (148.9 x 54.6 cm.); Nos. 82B, 82D, 82F, 58⅝ x 17⅞ in. (148.9 x 45.4 cm.). Painted perhaps in the 1730s.

COLLECTIONS: du Sommerard; Morgan; Duveen; Frick (1916).

Although they are presently mounted to serve as a screen, the panels probably were painted as room decorations and may have formed part of a larger suite representing the months of the year. They have been attributed to Lajoue on the basis of their resemblance to that artist's engraved designs and decorative paintings, which have similarly asymmetric compositions and employ as decorative motifs a profusion of shells, canopies, trellises, and consoles.

GEORGES DE LA TOUR   1593 – 1652

Most of La Tour's life was spent in his native Lorraine, although his style — which appears to have been influenced by Caravaggio or by his Dutch followers, such as Honthorst — suggests that the artist may have traveled abroad. La Tour evidently worked for Louis XIII, inasmuch as a document refers to him as "Peintre Ordinaire du Roy." He also received various commissions from the ducal court of Lorraine.

The Education of the Virgin   (48.1.155)

Oil, on canvas, 33 x 39½ in. (83.8 x 100.4 cm.). Signed: *de la Tour f.* Painted about 1650.

COLLECTIONS: Robert; Knoedler; Frick (1948).

La Tour's striking use of light transfigures simple genre motifs, lending his scenes an air of mysterious significance. Closely similar paintings of the education of the Virgin by St. Anne, a theme which first appears in fifteenth-century illuminated manuscripts, exist in several collections, and all the known versions may be workshop replicas of a lost original by La Tour.

SIR THOMAS LAWRENCE   1769 – 1830

Lawrence, born in Bristol, was appointed Painter to the King at the age of twenty-two. He was elected to the Royal Academy in 1794 and later became its President.

Julia, Lady Peel   (04.1.83)

Oil, on canvas, 35¾ x 27⅞ in. (90.8 x 70.8 cm.). Painted in 1827.
COLLECTIONS: Peel; Bardac; Knoedler; Frick (1904).

Julia Floyd (1795–1859) was the wife of the famous statesman Sir Robert Peel, who was an enthusiastic patron of Lawrence's. This portrait apparently was inspired by Rubens' *Chapeau de paille*, a portrait of the artist's wife, which Peel had acquired in 1823.

Miss Louisa Murray   (16.1.84)

Oil, on canvas, 36½ x 28⅞ in. (92.7 x 73.3 cm.). Painted probably after 1827.
COLLECTIONS: Sedelmeyer; Elkington; Wanamaker; Bacon; Frick (1916).

Of the several versions of Lawrence's portrait of Louisa Georgina Murray (1822–91), that in the Iveagh Collection (Kenwood, London) is considered the original. The Frick version is probably a studio copy painted after 1827. (Not illustrated.)

FRA FILIPPO LIPPI   c. 1406 – 1469

Born in Florence, Fra Filippo took the monastic vows of the Carmelite Order in 1421. He was in Padua in 1434, but three years later he returned to Florence, where he was employed by the Medici and other prominent families. He died at Spoleto, where he had gone to execute frescoes in the Cathedral.

The Annunciation   (24.1.85)

Tempera, on poplar panels: left panel, 25⅛ x 9⅞ in. (63.8 x 25.1 cm.); right panel, 25⅛ x 10 in. (63.8 x 25.4 cm.). Painted about 1440.
COLLECTIONS: Calcagno; Langton Douglas; Frick (1924).

In Florentine art of the mid-fifteenth century the subject of the Annunciation was exceedingly popular, and Fra Filippo depicted it in many paintings. The lily carried by the angel Gabriel in these pictures symbolizes the purity of the Virgin, while the dove indicates the angel's words to her: "The Holy Ghost shall come upon thee." The two Frick panels, now framed together, probably once formed wings on either side of an altarpiece.

ÉDOUARD MANET 1832–1883

Born in Paris, Manet studied with Couture for six years, during which time he also traveled extensively. In 1861 he exhibited for the first time in the Salon, but in 1863 he was among those showing at the Salon des Refusés, where his work provoked violent ridicule. During most of his career Manet faced hostile criticism and public antipathy. He was, however, defended by Baudelaire and Zola, and official recognition finally came to him the year before his death, when he was awarded the Legion of Honor.

The Bullfight (14.1.86)

Oil, on canvas, 18⅞ x 42⅞ in. (47.9 x 108.9 cm.). Signed: M. Painted in 1864.

COLLECTIONS: Vitta; Dunn; Knoedler; Frick (1914).

The picture originally formed the upper part of a canvas entitled *An Incident in the Bullring*, which Manet exhibited in the Salon of 1864. After the Salon, possibly because of biting reviews and caricatures of the painting, Manet cut out two separate compositions from the canvas, discarding a middle strip and a segment at the upper left. The lower, larger section, now known as *The Dead Toreador*, is in the National Gallery, Washington. The Spanish subjects that appear frequently in Manet's work in the 1860s attest to his enthusiasm both for Spain and for the art of Velázquez and Goya.

JACOBUS HENDRIKUS MARIS
1837 – 1899

Maris was born and trained in The Hague. During the late 1860s he was in Paris, where he was influenced by the landscapes of the Barbizon painters. After his return to Holland in 1871 he became a leading figure in The Hague school of painting, together with his brothers Matthijs and Willem.

The Bridge   (14.1.87)

Oil, on canvas, 44⅜ x 54⅜ in. (112.7 x 138.1 cm.). Signed: *J. Maris.* Painted in 1885.

COLLECTIONS: Forbes; Young; Knoedler; Frick; Knoedler; Dunn; Colnaghi and Knoedler; Frick (1914).

The site represented is said to be near Rijswijk, outside The Hague. An impression of Maris' etching of the same subject, somewhat simplified, is also in The Frick Collection. Van Gogh, who frequently mentioned Maris in his letters, was influenced by paintings of this type during his formative years in Holland.

HANS MEMLING   c. 1440 – 1494

Born at Seligenstadt, near Frankfurt, Memling spent much of his life in Bruges, where he was recorded as a new citizen in 1465. Two years later he entered the painters' guild of Bruges, and documents indicate that he became a prosperous citizen of that city. Although certain elements in his paintings recall Rogier van der Weyden, there is no proof that Rogier was Memling's teacher. In addition to portraits, Memling painted many religious subjects.

Portrait of a Man   (68.1.169)

Oil, on oak panel, 13⅛ x 9⅛ in. (33.5 x 23.2 cm.).
COLLECTIONS: van der Elst; Frick (1968).

Although panels such as this often were intended as covers or wings for small private altarpieces, during the second half of the fifteenth century the demand for portraits as freestanding works of art increased rapidly, and it seems likely that this representation of an unidentified man was commissioned as an independent painting. Memling was one of the most admired portraitists of his day, in Italy as well as in Northern Europe. His popularity was due not only to his great skill in representing a physical likeness, but also to his even rarer ability to convey a sense of the intellectual and spiritual character of his subjects.

GABRIEL METSU   1629–1667

Metsu was born in Leyden and lived there at least until 1654, but by 1657 he had moved to Amsterdam. He painted genre scenes, small portraits, and religious subjects, and appears to have been influenced by Flemish painters, by ter Borch, and by members of the Delft school, especially de Hoogh and Vermeer.

A Lady at Her Toilet   (05.1.88)

Oil, on canvas, 20⅜ x 16⅝ in. (51.7 x 42.2 cm.). Signed: *G Metsu*. Painted about 1660.

COLLECTIONS: Lormier; Hope; Clinton-Hope; Colnaghi and Wertheimer; Lawrie; Knoedler; Frick (1905).

In Amsterdam Metsu painted a number of interior scenes inspired, as is this one, by the work of ter Borch in their modest scale, finely painted detail, and richness of handling. The foreground figure in particular displays the polished technique characteristic of Metsu. Although his paintings brought Metsu only modest success during his lifetime, they were highly prized by eighteenth-century collectors.

JEAN-FRANÇOIS MILLET 1814–1875

The son of Norman peasants, Millet studied first in Cherbourg and later in Paris. His work was shown in several Salons in the 1840s, but it was not until 1848 that he began to exhibit the peasant subjects that ultimately made him famous. In 1849 he moved to Barbizon, where he spent most of his remaining years.

Woman Sewing by Lamplight (06.1.89)

Oil, on canvas, 39⅜ x 32¼ in. (100.7 x 81.9 cm.). Signed: *J. F. Millet.* Painted 1870–72.

COLLECTIONS: Durand-Ruel; Laurent-Richard; Durand-Ruel; Tabourier; Smit; Cottier; Frick (1906).

Millet's fondness for ancient Roman bucolic poetry may have influenced his choice of this subject. The woman sewing, a motif that recurs often in his work, seems to recall certain passages from Virgil's *Georgics*, translated into Norman peasant settings. Though finished in Barbizon in 1872, the Frick canvas was begun in Cherbourg, where Millet's family had moved temporarily to escape the invading Prussian armies.

CLAUDE-OSCAR MONET 1840 – 1926

Though born in Paris, Monet spent his youth in Le Havre, where he worked with the painter Boudin. He returned to Paris in 1862, exhibited in the Salons of 1865 and 1866, and visited England and Holland in the early 1870s. With Bazille, Monet organized the first Impressionist exhibition of 1874, which included works by Renoir, Pissarro, Sisley, Cézanne, and Degas. Monet painted in many parts of France, as well as in Holland and Venice. During his last years he worked chiefly in his own gardens at Giverny.

Vétheuil in Winter   (42.1.146)

Oil, on canvas, 27 x 35⅜ in. (68 x 89.4 cm.). Signed: *Claude Monet.* Painted in 1879 or 1880.

COLLECTIONS: Staub-Terlinden; Wildenstein; Frick (1942).

In 1878 Monet moved to Vétheuil, a small town on the river Seine, which he painted from many different prospects and in every season. The Frick canvas, executed almost entirely in blues and blue-greens with touches of rose tinting the snow and houses, vividly conveys an impression of the intense cold that occurred during the severe winter of 1879–80.

JEAN-MARC NATTIER 1685 – 1766

Nattier studied at the Academy and was already a portraitist of note by the age of eighteen. In 1717 Peter the Great summoned him to Holland, where he painted members of the visiting Russian court. The following year he was received into the Academy in Paris. Nattier exhibited frequently in the Salons and received many commissions from the French royal court.

Elizabeth, Countess of Warwick (99.1.90)

Oil, on canvas, 32⅛ x 25¾ in. (81.5 x 65.4 cm.). Signed and dated: *Nattier | p.x. 1754.*

COLLECTIONS: Warwick; Greville; Finch-Hatton; Lawrie; Frick (1899).

Elizabeth (d. 1800), daughter of Lord Archibald Hamilton, married Francis Greville, later Earl of Warwick, in 1742. On hearing of their engagement, Horace Walpole wrote, "She is excessively pretty and sensible, but as diminutive as he." Nattier also painted portraits of her husband. The composition of the Frick painting is simple and restrained in comparison to the opulent and frequently allegorical portraits with which the artist is generally associated.

ISACK VAN OSTADE   1621 – 1649

Van Ostade was born in Haarlem and worked there throughout his short life. He studied with his older brother Adriaen, whose scenes of peasant cottages and taverns were the chief inspiration for his early work. Isack, a prolific painter, later turned to outdoor genre subjects and winter landscapes.

Travelers Halting at an Inn   (07.1.91)

Oil, on oak panel, 20⅛ x 24½ in. (51.1 x 62.2 cm.). Signed: *Isack. Ostade.*

COLLECTIONS: Leuchtenberg; Knoedler; Frick (1907).

Van Ostade, like his brother Adriaen and other Haarlem painters, was attracted by the picturesque animation of country inns. He treated aspects of the subject many times, typically in landscapes enriched by subtle effects of silvery daylight.

JEAN-BAPTISTE PATER   1695–1736

Born in Valenciennes, Pater received his artistic training from his fellow townsman Jean-Antoine Watteau, whom he accompanied to Paris around 1710. The two eventually parted because of temperamental differences, but in 1721 Watteau, mortally ill, made peace with Pater, who appears to have inherited his unfinished paintings and some commissions. Pater was elected to the Academy in 1728 as a painter of fêtes galantes.

Procession of Italian Comedians   (18.1.92)

Oil, on canvas, 29¼ x 23⅜ in. (74.3 x 59.4 cm.).
COLLECTIONS: Pembroke; Duveen; Frick (1918).

Though this painting and *The Village Orchestra* (see following entry) seem to have been regarded as pendants as early as 1739, they have no precise iconographic relationship. The stock characters who appear in the *Procession* — including Pierrot, the Doctor, and Columbine — recur frequently in the art and literature of Pater's day. They were popularized by the roving troupes of Italian *commedia dell'arte* players who had been banished from France by Louis XIV but returned to enjoy great popular success after his death.

PATER

The Village Orchestra (18.1.93)

Oil, on canvas, 29⅜ x 23½ in. (74.6 x 59.7 cm.).
COLLECTIONS: See preceding entry.

In contrast to the associations with theatrical tradition evoked by the *Procession* (see preceding entry), *The Village Orchestra* recalls more contemporary aspects of life in eighteenth-century France — in particular the musical diversions of country fairs. The elegant figures and polished technique that distinguish both these canvases are a testimony of Pater's debt to his master, Watteau, to whom the paintings once were attributed.

PIERO DELLA FRANCESCA   1410/20–1492

Piero was born in Borgo Sansepolcro and during the course of his life received several commissions for altarpieces from that town. He is first recorded in 1439 as working in Florence with Domenico Veneziano. In 1451 he painted a fresco for Sigismondo Malatesta in Rimini, and the following year he began the fresco cycle of the Legend of the True Cross in the church of S. Francesco, Arezzo. Piero's art reflects his intense interest in the theoretical study of perspective and geometry.

St. Simon the Apostle (?)   (36.1.138)

Tempera, on poplar panel, 52¾ x 24½ in. (134 x 62.2 cm.). Painted probably between 1454 and 1469.

COLLECTIONS: Church of S. Agostino, Borgo Sansepolcro; Cardona (?); Austrian Imperial Academy at Milan (?); Miller zu Aicholz; Knoedler; Frick (1936).

In 1454 Angelo di Giovanni di Simone d'Angelo commissioned from Piero della Francesca an altarpiece for S. Agostino in Borgo Sansepolcro. It was to include several panels with "images, figures, pictures, and ornaments." The central portion,

perhaps a Coronation of the Virgin, is lost, but the four wing panels with standing saints—St. Simon(?), St. Michael the Archangel, St. Augustine, and St. Nicholas of Tolentino — have survived. Although the venerable figure in the Frick painting bears no identifying attributes, he is thought to represent St. Simon the Apostle, as Simon was the patron saint of the donor's deceased brother Simone. The steps that appear in the lower left of the Frick panel may be a continuation of the base of a throne from the lost central panel; steps also appear at lower right in the St. Michael panel.

PIERO DELLA FRANCESCA, Workshop of

Augustinian Monk   (50.1.157)

Tempera, on poplar panel, 15¾ x 11⅛ in. (40 x 28.2 cm.).

Augustinian Nun   (50.1.158)

Tempera, on poplar panel, 15¼ x 11 in. (38.7 x 27.9 cm.).
COLLECTIONS: Church of S. Agostino, Borgo Sansepolcro (?);
Franceschi-Marini; Liechtenstein; Knoedler; Frick (1950).

These two panels and a related panel of *St. Apollonia* in the
National Gallery, Washington, are believed to be subsidiary
parts of Piero's S. Agostino altarpiece (see preceding entry).
This assumption is supported by the fact that the dark gray
habits in the Frick panels are clearly Augustinian, and that S.
Agostino was the only Augustinian church in Borgo Sansepolcro, the town where the paintings remained until about 1900.
The smaller panels of altarpieces often were executed by assistants, as was probably the case with these two works.

CAREL VAN DER PLUYM 1625 – 1672

Van der Pluym was born and lived in Leyden, where his family were official city plumbers, and where the artist was a charter member of the painters' guild in 1648. He was a cousin to Rembrandt, with whom he may have studied and whose style he emulated.

Old Woman with a Book (16.1.99)

Oil, on canvas, 38⅝ x 30¾ in. (98.1 x 78.1 cm.).
COLLECTIONS: Fraula; Beeckmans; Leith; Ross; Sedelmeyer; Porgès; Frick (1916).

As were many depictions of old women painted in the style of Rembrandt, this canvas was once believed to be a portrait by Rembrandt of his mother. However, the coloring and technique of modeling more closely resemble those of signed works by van der Pluym.

SIR HENRY RAEBURN   1756 – 1823

When barely in his twenties, Raeburn had already established himself as a miniaturist in Edinburgh. Between 1785 and 1787 he worked in Rome on the advice of Reynolds, and soon after his return to Edinburgh he became the leading Scottish portraitist. He was elected to the Royal Academy in 1815 and named His Majesty's Limner for Scotland in 1822.

James Cruikshank   (11.1.94)

Oil, on canvas, 50 x 40 in. (127 x 101.6 cm.). Painted probably about 1805–08.

COLLECTIONS: Cruikshank; Agnew; Forbes and Paterson; Sedelmeyer; Kann; Knoedler; Frick (1911).

James Cruikshank of Langley Park, Montrose, Forfarshire, was a businessman who made a large fortune in the island of St. Vincent, British West Indies. In 1792 he married Margaret Helen, daughter of the Rev. Alexander Gerard of Rochsoles, Lanarkshire. She died in 1823, her husband in 1830.

Mrs. James Cruikshank   (05.1.95)

Oil, on canvas, 50¾ x 40 in. (128.9 x 101.6 cm.). Painted probably about 1805-08.

COLLECTIONS: Cruikshank; Agnew; Sanderson; Holms; Knoedler; Frick (1905).

No record of the commission for the portraits of Mrs. Cruikshank and her husband (see preceding entry) has been found, but a dating of 1805–08 has been suggested on stylistic grounds. The portraits were separated for many years until their reunion in The Frick Collection in 1911.

REMBRANDT HARMENSZ. VAN RIJN
1606 – 1669

Born in Leyden, Rembrandt studied there and later worked in Amsterdam under the history painter Pieter Lastman. He returned to Leyden, where he taught his first pupils, then in 1631/32 he moved permanently to Amsterdam, quickly achieving popular success as a painter of single and group portraits, Biblical scenes, and historical subjects. Despite his fame and his many pupils, Rembrandt suffered a series of financial difficulties that led to insolvency in 1656. By 1660, however, most of his debts were settled, and he spent his last years in relative comfort.

Nicolaes Ruts   (43.1.150)

Oil, on mahogany panel, 46 x 34⅜ in. (116.8 x 87.3 cm.). Signed and dated: R[H?]L. 1631.

COLLECTIONS: Ruts; Romswinckel; Meynts; Willem II of the Netherlands; Weimar; Hope; Agnew; Ruston; Colnaghi; Boni de Castellane; Morgan; Knoedler; Frick (1943).

Ruts (1573–1638) was an Amsterdam merchant who traded with Russia, no doubt the source of the rich furs he wears in this painting. Perhaps the first portrait commission Rembrandt received from outside his own family, the picture must have contributed to his quick rise to fame. The dramatic contrasts in lighting and the detailed rendering of varied textures are characteristic of Rembrandt's early works, differing markedly from the warm, diffused light and broad brushwork of his *Self-Portrait* (see later entry) painted more than a quarter of a century afterward.

REMBRANDT

The Polish Rider

(10.1.98)

Oil, on canvas, 46 x 53⅛ in. (116.8 x 134.9 cm.). Signed *R[e?]*. Painted about 1655.

COLLECTIONS: Oginski; Stanislaus II Augustus of Poland; Tyszkiewicz; Drucki-Lubecki; Stroynowski; Tarnowski; Frick (1910).

This enigmatic representation of a youth riding resolutely through a shadowy landscape has evoked many interpretations. Scholars agree that Rembrandt painted it about 1655, and that it ranks among his most impressive and moving works, but its subject matter and meaning remain in doubt. It is not a conventional equestrian portrait, nor does it appear to represent any specific historical or literary figure. Rembrandt may have intended it as a glorification of the latter-day Christian knights who in the painter's time were still defending Eastern Europe against the Turks.

REMBRANDT

Self-Portrait (06.1.97)

Oil, on canvas, 52⅝ x 40⅞ in. (133.7 x 103.8 cm.). Signed and dated: *Rembrandt | f. 1658*.

COLLECTIONS: Ilchester; Knoedler; Frick (1906).

Rembrandt painted more than sixty self-portraits and drew and etched his own likeness repeatedly. These self-portraits range from early works that often served as experiments in dramatic lighting effects or transitory facial expressions, to the more subtle and searching images of his later years. The Frick canvas, with its psychological depth, monumental design, and rich, warm coloring, is surely the most imposing of the self-portraits. The artist, poor and burdened with personal problems, depicted himself — in poignant and perhaps ironic contrast — with the splendid costume and enthroned dignity of an Oriental monarch.

REMBRANDT

Portrait of a Young Artist   (99.1.96)

Oil, on canvas, 39⅛ x 35 in. (99.4 x 88.9 cm.). Spurious signature
and date: *Rembrandt f: / 164[7?]*.

COLLECTIONS: Aved; Carlisle; Colnaghi; Tooth; Frick (1899).

The subject of this portrait remains unidentified, although he
has variously been called Leonaert Bramer, Carel Fabritius,
Jan van de Cappelle, and Jan Asselyn. The painting is in the
style of Rembrandt's portraits of the late 1640s, but it could
well be the work of a Rembrandt pupil. The acquisition of
this canvas in 1899 marked a turning point in the formation of
Mr. Frick's collection; his earlier purchases had been limited
almost exclusively to works by contemporary Salon painters
and members of the Barbizon School.

PIERRE-AUGUSTE RENOIR   1841 – 1919

Renoir began his career as a painter of porcelain in Limoges, then studied with Gleyre in Paris. He first exhibited in the Salon of 1864, and ten years later he was among those who organized the first Impressionist exhibition. After trips to Algeria and Italy in 1881, Renoir's work began to diverge from that of the Impressionists.

Mother and Children   (14.1.100)

Oil, on canvas, 67 x 42⅜ in. (170.2 x 108.3 cm.). Signed: *Renoir*. Painted about 1874–76.

COLLECTIONS: Paulin; Palmer; Durand-Ruel; Knoedler; Frick (1914).

In 1876 Renoir rented a new studio at the top of Montmartre, possibly with funds he received in payment for this portrait of an unidentified young mother walking her children in a park. Such pleasing portraits brought Renoir success at a time when his fellow Impressionists were finding difficulty in selling their works. While large-scale foreground figures recur frequently in

the artist's compositions, the silhouetting of the sapphire blue area of the mother's coat against the soft, pale blues and violets of the background is especially characteristic of Renoir's work in the mid-1870s.

SIR JOSHUA REYNOLDS 1723 – 1792

After an apprenticeship under Thomas Hudson, Reynolds began his career as a portraitist in Plymouth. Between 1749 and 1752 he was in Italy, where the study of ancient art and the Italian masters profoundly influenced his style. In 1768 he became the first president of the Royal Academy. The "Discourses" he delivered at the Academy in subsequent years exerted a significant influence on the development of British aesthetic theory.

General John Burgoyne (43.1.149)

Oil, on canvas, 50 x 39⅞ in. (127 x 101.3 cm.). Painted probably in 1766.

COLLECTIONS: La Lippe(?); Schaumburg-Lippe; Rusch; Morgan; Knoedler; Frick (1943).

Best remembered as the general dramatically defeated by American forces at Saratoga, John Burgoyne (1722–92) was also a Member of Parliament, a dandy, a gambler, and an amateur actor and dramatist. This portrait may have been commissioned by Burgoyne's senior officer, Count La Lippe, as a memento of their campaigns in Spain and Portugal. Burgoyne's uniform is that of the Sixteenth Light Dragoons as it was worn before May 1766.

REYNOLDS

Elizabeth, Lady Taylor (10.1.101)

Oil, on canvas, 50⅛ x 40¼ in. (127.3 x 102.2 cm.). Painted about 1780.

COLLECTIONS: Wertheimer; Sedelmeyer; Kann; Duveen; Frick (1910).

The subject of this portrait has been tentatively identified as Elizabeth Goodin Houghton (d.1831), who married Sir John Taylor in 1778. The hurried, often illegible entries in Reynolds' notebooks make it difficult to assign specific dates to many of his portraits, but the costume worn by Lady Taylor suggests a date in the late 1770s or early 1780s.

REYNOLDS

Selina, Lady Skipwith

(06.1.102)

Oil, on canvas, 50½ x 40¼ in. (128.3 x 102.2 cm.). Painted in 1787.
COLLECTIONS: Skipwith; Knoedler; Frick (1906).

Selina (1752–1832), eldest daughter of the Hon. George Shirley of Eattington, Warwickshire, was married in 1785 to Sir Thomas George Skipwith of Newbold Hall, Warwickshire. Reynolds' notebooks state that her portrait was painted in May of 1787. The natural pose and setting, as well as the fresh, free handling of paint, are typical of Reynolds' late style.

GEORGE ROMNEY 1734–1802

Before moving to London in 1762, Romney had studied and achieved some success as a portrait painter in the north of England. He visited Paris in 1764, and in 1773 he began a two-year sojourn in Italy. Romney was a prolific artist who rivaled Reynolds as a fashionable portraitist. In 1799 he retired to Kendal, where he died.

Miss Frances Mary Harford   (03.1.105)

> Oil, on canvas, 30 x 25¼ in. (76.2 x 64.1 cm.). Painted between 1780 and 1783.
>
> COLLECTIONS: Egremont; Colnaghi; Lawrie; Coats; Knoedler; Frick (1903).

Frances Harford was the natural daughter of Frederick Calvert, seventh Lord Baltimore, from whom she inherited considerable wealth. At the age of thirteen she was married to her guardian, Robert Morris, but this union was declared void twelve years later; she then married the Hon. William Frederick Wyndham, son of the Earl of Egremont. To judge from the number of sittings recorded in Romney's diary, the artist must have executed three or four portraits of Miss Harford.

ROMNEY

Lady Hamilton as 'Nature'   (04.1.103)

Oil, on canvas, 29⅞ x 24¾ in. (75.8 x 62.8 cm.). Painted in 1782.
COLLECTIONS: Greville; Hamilton; Parker; Fawkes; Wertheimer;
Cronier; Knoedler; Frick (1904).

Emma Lyon (1765–1815), who later in life called herself Emily
Hart, was the daughter of a Cheshire blacksmith. A fascinating
personality and beauty, she was in turn the mistress of Charles
Greville, who commissioned this portrait, of Sir William Hamilton, Greville's uncle and British envoy to Naples, whom she
married in 1791, and of Lord Nelson, with whom she lived until his death in 1805. She died in poverty in Calais. During the
height of her social success Lady Hamilton was famous for her
"attitudes" — a kind of romantic aesthetic posturing. Romney
painted more than twenty portraits of her, several in the guise
of characters from history, mythology, and literature.

ROMNEY

Henrietta, Countess of Warwick, and Her Children

(08.1.107)

Oil, on canvas, 79¾ x 61½ in. (202.6 x 156.2 cm.). Painted 1787–89.
COLLECTIONS: Warwick; Knoedler; Frick (1908).

Henrietta Vernon (1760–1838) was the second wife of George Greville, Earl of Warwick. Horace Walpole mentioned Henrietta and her sisters in his letters and also wrote verses to them. Romney has depicted her with two of her children, Sir Henry Richard and Lady Elizabeth, in this composition recalling the group portraits Van Dyck executed in England.

ROMNEY

Miss Mary Finch-Hatton (98.1.104)

Oil, on canvas, 29⅞ x 25⅛ in. (75.8 x 63.8 cm.). Painted in 1788.
COLLECTIONS: Finch-Hatton; Knoedler; Frick (1898).

Mary Finch-Hatton, the daughter of John Finch-Hatton of
Long Stanton Hall, near Cambridge, married Hale Wortham
of Royston, Hertfordshire. Romney's notebooks record six
sittings for Miss Finch-Hatton. The bold and summary brushwork evident in this portrait resembles the technique of Romney's numerous wash drawings.

ROMNEY

Charlotte, Lady Milnes (11.1.106)

Oil, on canvas, 95⅛ x 58¾ in. (241.6 x 149.2 cm.). Painted 1788–92.
COLLECTIONS: Milnes; Crewe; Duveen; Frick (1911).

Charlotte Frances (1767/68–1850), daughter of Capt. John
Albert Bentinck, R. N., of Terrington St. Clements, Norfolk,
was married in 1785 to Robert Shore Milnes. Her husband
had been a patron of Romney, and in 1788 he commissioned
from the artist this rather classicizing portrait, as well as one
of himself which is now at Helperby Hall, Helperby, York.

PIERRE-ÉTIENNE-THÉODORE ROUSSEAU 1812 – 1867

Rousseau was born and trained in Paris, where he was much influenced by the Dutch landscapes in the Louvre. Although he began exhibiting at the Salon in 1831, he had little success until 1849, when he won a first-class medal and considerable public acclaim. After 1848 he settled in the village of Barbizon with Millet, Daubigny, and others of the group that came to be known as the Barbizon School.

The Village of Becquigny   (02.1.108)

Oil, on mahogany panel, 25 x 39⅜ in. (63.5 x 100 cm.). Signed: *TH. Rousseau*. Begun about 1857.

COLLECTIONS: Hartmann; Coats; Knoedler; Frick (1902).

During the last ten years of his life Rousseau reworked many times this panel representing a village in Picardy, a composition that clearly recalls Dutch seventeenth-century landscapes. The day before sending it to the Salon of 1864 he altered the sky to a bright sapphire blue, in imitation of Japanese prints, but the sky was so widely criticized that the artist eventually restored the softer blues of the earlier version. Rousseau's friends considered this painting one of his most important and successful landscapes.

PETER PAUL RUBENS, Follower of
Seventeenth Century

Sir Peter Paul Rubens (1577–1640), who worked in Italy, Spain, England, and France as well as in his native Flanders, directed an extensive workshop employing numerous assistants. His style influenced many contemporaries in Flanders and throughout Europe.

A Knight of the Order of
the Golden Fleece   (15.1.109)

Oil, on canvas, 39¾ x 30½ in. (101 x 77.5 cm.).
COLLECTIONS: von Renesse-Breitbach; Knoedler; Frick (1915).

The unidentified subject of this portrait wears the gold chain and insignia of the Order of the Golden Fleece. The painting was ascribed formerly to Rubens himself, and later, with insufficient evidence, to Van Dyck, to Snyders, and to Cornelis de Vos, all collaborators of Rubens. Another version of the portrait is in the New York Historical Society.

JACOB VAN RUISDAEL   1628/29 – 1682

Ruisdael was born in Haarlem and was admitted to the painters'
guild there in 1648, presumably after studying with his uncle,
Salomon van Ruysdael. By 1657 he was living in Amsterdam,
where he seems to have spent the rest of his life. His dated paint-
ings range from 1646 to 1678. Ruisdael's paintings, drawings,
and etchings are devoted entirely to landscape.

Landscape with a Footbridge   (49.1.156)

Oil, on canvas, 38¾ x 62⅝ in. (98.4 x 159.1 cm.). Signed and dated:
JRuisdael 1652.

COLLECTIONS: Wombwell (?); von Rothschild; Rosenberg and
Stiebel; Frick (1949).

In 1650 Ruisdael traveled to the hilly border region of eastern
Holland and made drawings there of scenery that contrasts
sharply with the flat land of the west, the chief subject of the
earlier Haarlem landscapists. Although only in his early twenties, Ruisdael shows in this painting a special talent for captur-
ing subtle effects of light, evident in the pale sun that filters
through the clouds dappling the landscape and reflecting from
the surface of the stream.

RUISDAEL

Quay at Amsterdam

(10.1.110)

Oil, on canvas, 20⅜ x 25⅞ in. (51.7 x 65.7 cm.). Signed: *J Ruisdael*.
Painted about 1670.

COLLECTIONS: de Beurnonville; Sedelmeyer; Kann; Duveen;
Frick (1910).

This rare urban scene by Ruisdael shows in the foreground the
north end of the Dam, the main square of Amsterdam, and
beyond it the broad canal called the Damrak (now filled). To
the right is the tower of the Oude Kerk. The artist included
this same site in a panorama of Amsterdam representing the
city from a bird's-eye view.

SALOMON VAN RUYSDAEL   1600 (?) – 1670

Salomon van Ruysdael was the uncle and perhaps the teacher of Jacob van Ruisdael. Born in Naarden, he became in 1623 a member of the painters' guild at Haarlem, where he remained until his death. While his earliest landscapes were influenced by Esaias van de Velde, many of his later works have affinities with those of Jan van Goyen.

River Scene: Men Dragging a Net   (05.1.111)

Oil, on canvas, 26¼ x 35⅛ in. (66.7 x 89.2 cm.). Painted about 1667.

COLLECTIONS: Ráth; Knoedler; Frick (1905).

The town in the background of this painting has been identified as Weesp, a community not far from Amsterdam. A riverbank, fishermen, boats, and a town in the distance are basic pictorial elements that the artist varied and rearranged repeatedly all his life. Here they are combined with particularly fine effects of sunset reflecting from the water.

GILBERT STUART 1755 – 1828

Stuart was born in Rhode Island. After studying in Scotland and working in London under Benjamin West, he returned to America in the early 1790s to become the leading American portraitist of his day. Stuart painted chiefly in New York, Philadelphia, and Boston.

George Washington   (18.1.112)

Oil, on canvas, 29¼ x 24 in. (74.3 x 60.9 cm.). Painted 1795–96.
COLLECTIONS: Camperdown; Knoedler; Frick (1918).

The artist gained a fortune from commissions for replicas of his various portraits of the first American President. The Frick canvas is thought to be a copy Stuart painted for John Vaughan of Philadelphia and belongs to the group known as the "Vaughan type," though it differs from other members of the group both in the color of the coat and in the background. Stylistically the portrait recalls the work of Stuart's English contemporaries, such as Romney and Hoppner.

GIOVANNI BATTISTA TIEPOLO
1696 – 1770

Tiepolo, a Venetian, was the leading Italian exponent of the rococo style. He executed numerous oil paintings and decorative frescoes for churches, palaces, and villas in Venice and north Italy, and he also worked at Würzburg and in Madrid, where he died. His art derives in part from that of his Venetian contemporaries and his sixteenth-century predecessor Veronese.

Perseus and Andromeda   (18.1.114)

Oil, on paper affixed to canvas, 20⅜ x 16 in. (51.8 x 40.6 cm.). Painted probably in 1730.

COLLECTIONS: Sedelmeyer; de la Rochebousseau; Parissot; Trotti; Knoedler; Frick (1918).

Tiepolo has represented the moment in ancient Greek myth when the hero Perseus rescues Andromeda from the rocks on which she was to have been sacrificed to a sea monster. The painting is a study for one of the ceiling frescoes (destroyed by bombing in 1943) in the Palazzo Archinto, Milan. Its spectacular perspective and luminous colors are typical of Tiepolo's decorative compositions.

119

JACOPO ROBUSTI (IL TINTORETTO),
Circle of

Jacopo Tintoretto (1518–94) is best known for his religious paintings commissioned by Venetian churches and scuole, *but he also painted portraits and executed mythological and allegorical cycles. The artist maintained a large workshop, which included his sons Domenico and Marco as well as his daughter Marietta; they perpetuated his style well into the seventeenth century.*

Portrait of a Venetian Procurator (38.1.142)

Oil, on canvas, 44⅝ x 35 in. (113.3 x 88.9 cm.).
COLLECTIONS: Abercorn; Duveen; Frick (1938).

The crimson robes, black cap, and black stole worn by the unknown subject of this portrait identify him as a Procurator of St. Mark. Seen in the background is the island of S. Giorgio Maggiore. Since the architecture depicted on the island does not include Palladio's church of S. Giorgio, the cornerstone of which was laid in 1566, it is assumed that the portrait or its prototype was painted before the mid-1560s.

TIZIANO VECELLIO (TITIAN)
1477/90 – 1576

Titian was born in Pieve di Cadore, in the Dolomite Alps; the date of his birth is a matter of controversy. He succeeded Giovanni Bellini, under whom he had studied, as painter to the Republic of Venice, and he also enjoyed the patronage of many of the leading courts of Europe, serving as official painter to the Emperor Charles V and to Charles' son, Philip II of Spain. He died in Venice in the Great Plague of 1576.

Portrait of a Man in a Red Cap   (15.1.116)

Oil, on canvas, 32⅜ x 28 in. (82.3 x 71.1 cm.). Painted about 1516.
COLLECTIONS: Methuen (?); Rogers; Edgell; Lane; Grenfell; Lane; Frick (1915).

This portrait of an unidentified young man is an early work of Titian. The contemplative mood of the subject and the diffused and gentle play of light over broadly painted surfaces are strongly reminiscent of Giorgione, to whom the canvas has occasionally been attributed.

TITIAN

Pietro Aretino (05.1.115)

Oil, on canvas, 40⅛ x 33¾ in. (102 x 85.7 cm.). Painted probably between 1548 and the early 1550s.

COLLECTIONS: Savelli(?); Chigi; Colnaghi; Knoedler; Frick (1905).

Aretino (1492–1556), writer of scurrilous verses, lives of saints, comedies, tragedies, and innumerable letters, also achieved considerable wealth and influence through literary flattery and blackmail. He was a close friend of Titian, who painted several portraits of him. In the Frick portrait, Titian conveys a sense of Aretino's intellectual power through the keen, forceful head, and of his worldliness through the solid, rounded mass of the richly robed figure.

CONSTANT TROYON 1810 – 1865

Born in Sèvres, Troyon was in his youth associated with the land-scape painters of Barbizon, but after a trip to Holland in 1847 his style was much influenced by Dutch landscape and animal paint-ing. Troyon was extremely successful and had numerous follow-ers throughout Europe.

A Pasture in Normandy   (99.1.117)

Oil, on panel, 17 x 25⅝ in. (43.2 x 65.1 cm.). Signed: C. TROYON. Painted in the 1850s.

COLLECTIONS: Roederer; Knoedler; Frick (1899).

The Frick landscape clearly recalls the work of such Dutch painters as Cuyp and Potter. In turn, its precise evocation of light and atmosphere suggests that Troyon may have influ-enced the landscape painting of the Impressionists.

JOSEPH MALLORD WILLIAM TURNER
1775 – 1851

Turner, the son of a London barber, studied at the Royal Academy, to which he was granted full membership in 1802. Known initially as a watercolorist, he began exhibiting oils in the mid-1790s. Turner traveled extensively in England and on the Continent, making an immense number of sketches, many of which he later used as the basis for paintings and prints.

Fishing Boats Entering
Calais Harbor   (04.1.120)

Oil, on canvas, 29 x 38¾ in. (73.7 x 98.4 cm.). Painted about 1803.
COLLECTIONS: Drake; Coats; Knoedler; Frick (1904).

During the temporary Peace of Amiens in 1802, Turner left for his first voyage on the Continent. Several sketches he made during this trip served as studies for the Frick painting and for the larger *Calais Pier*, now in the National Gallery, London. The turbulent movement of the water and the dramatic sky recall Dutch seascapes of the seventeenth century.

TURNER

The Harbor of Dieppe (14.1.122)

Oil, on canvas, 68⅜ x 88¾ in. (173.7 x 225.4 cm.). Dated: *182[6?]*.
COLLECTIONS: Wadmore; Naylor; Agnew and Sulley; Knoedler;
Frick (1914).

Dieppe is the second of three large exhibition pieces Turner
painted representing northern Continental ports. The first,
Dordrecht (Paul Mellon collection), was exhibited at the Royal
Academy in 1818, and the third is The Frick Collection's
Cologne (see following entry). Sketches for *Dieppe* date from
the summer of 1821 and record a number of buildings that
are still to be seen in the city today. The composition recalls,
probably deliberately, Claude Lorrain's views of harbors with
a setting or rising sun.

TURNER

Cologne: The Arrival of a
Packet-Boat: Evening

(14.1.119)

Oil, and possibly watercolor, on canvas, 66⅜ x 88¼ in. (168.6 x 224.1 cm.). Painted in 1826.

COLLECTIONS: Broadhurst (?); Wadmore; Naylor; Agnew and Sulley; Knoedler; Frick (1914).

According to an account by Ruskin, Turner consented to darken this painting with lampblack during the Royal Academy exhibition of 1826 in order not to detract from two portraits by Lawrence which hung at either side of it. However, contemporary critical references to its "glitter and gaud of colors" as well as to the delicate nature of its surface medium cast doubt on Ruskin's anecdote. The canvas is based on sketches Turner made during tours along the Rhine in 1817 and 1825.

126

TURNER

Mortlake Terrace: Early
Summer Morning

(09.1.121)

Oil, on canvas, 36⅝ x 48½ in. (93 x 123.2 cm.). Painted in 1826.
COLLECTIONS: Moffatt; Hamatt; Allnutt; Fripp (?); Mendel;
Agnew; Price; Agnew; Holland; Knoedler; Mellon (?); Frick (1909).

Turner painted this canvas for William Moffatt, depicting in
it Moffatt's house at Mortlake, on the Thames not far from
London. As is usual with Turner, the painting is based on numerous preparatory drawings in which the artist recorded the
topography and studied various ways of balancing the house
and land against the river and sky. A companion piece — a view
of the estate on a summer evening — is now in the Mellon Collection, National Gallery, Washington. The Moffatt house still
stands at Mortlake.

127

TURNER

Antwerp: Van Goyen Looking Out for a Subject

Oil, on canvas, 36⅛ x 48⅜ in. (91.8 x 122.9 cm.). Painted in 1833. COLLECTIONS: Bicknell; Heugh; Agnew; Graham; Agnew; Henson; Guthrie; Agnew; Knoedler; Frick (1901).

The reference in the title to Jan van Goyen and the inscription VAN G. on the boat in the foreground identify the figure standing prominently in that boat as the seventeenth-century Dutch artist. Like Turner, van Goyen visited Antwerp and executed paintings on the basis of sketches he drew there. Turner made several allusions to seventeenth-century Dutch painters in the titles of his works — witness his *Rembrandt's Daughter* and *Port Ruysdael*.

TUSCAN SCHOOL   Late Thirteenth Century (?)

The Flagellation of Christ   (50.1.159)

Tempera, on poplar panel, 9¾ x 7⅞ in. (24.7 x 20 cm.).
COLLECTIONS: Rolla; Moratilla; Knoedler; Frick (1950).

The Frick panel, no doubt originally part of an altarpiece or
tabernacle, has provoked considerable scholarly discussion,
eliciting attributions to Duccio, to Cimabue, and to an unknown Tuscan artist influenced by both these masters. The
subject of the Flagellation was widely employed by Italian
artists during the second half of the thirteenth century and
also appears frequently in contemporary poetry and drama.
These same years saw numerous pilgrimages of penitents who,
in imitation of Christ's suffering, lashed themselves and one
another as they marched in procession.

DIEGO RODRÍGUEZ DE SILVA Y VELÁZQUEZ   1599 – 1660

Born in Seville, Velázquez was apprenticed there to Francisco Pacheco. In 1623 he was called to the service of Philip IV, who appointed him court painter and ennobled him. His early genre scenes reveal the influence of Caravaggio, and he also studied works by the Venetian painters in the royal collection and probably was influenced by Rubens during the latter's visit to Madrid in 1628–29. Apart from trips to Italy in 1629–31 and 1649, Velázquez remained at the Spanish court until his death.

King Philip IV of Spain   (11.1.123)

Oil, on canvas, 51⅛ x 39⅛ in. (129.8 x 99.4 cm.). Painted in 1644. COLLECTIONS: Royal family of Spain; Ducal family of Parma; Agnew; Knoedler with Scott and Fowles; Frick (1911).

Philip IV (1605–65), who succeeded to the Spanish throne in 1621, was a weak administrator and military commander but a great patron of the arts and letters. He promoted the Spanish theater, built the Palacio del Buen-Retiro in Madrid, enlarged the royal collections, and was Velázquez' most ardent sup-

porter. In 1644 Velázquez accompanied the King to Fraga, where the Spaniards won an important victory against the French. There, in a dilapidated, improvised studio, he painted this portrait, which represents the King in the costume he wore during the campaign.

PAOLO and GIOVANNI VENEZIANO

Paolo, Active 1321 – 1358

Paolo Veneziano is considered the leading figure of Venetian trecento *painting. Nothing is known of his son Giovanni beyond his participation in the Frick painting and in the painted cover for the Pala d'Oro in S. Marco, Venice (dated 1345).*

The Coronation of the Virgin (30.1.124)

Tempera, on poplar panel, 43¼ x 27 in. (110 x 68.5 cm.). Signed and dated: M.C.C.C.L.V.I.I.I. / PAVLVS CVM / IOHANINVS EIV̄ / FILIV̄ / PĪSERV̄T HOC OP.

COLLECTIONS: Chapel near Ravenna (?); Baccinetti; Maillinger; Reichardt; Prince of Hohenzollern-Sigmaringen; Knoedler; Frick (1930).

The Coronation of the Virgin is an event recounted not in the Bible, but in the apocryphal story of the Virgin's death. In many Coronation scenes painted by Paolo and other Venetian artists the sun and moon accompany the major figures, the sun from early times being associated with Christ and the moon with the Virgin. The inscription along the base of the

throne in the Frick painting contains the opening lines of the antiphon *Regina coeli,* and the angels singing and playing musical instruments symbolize the harmony of the universe. The angels' instruments are authentic components of the medieval orchestra, and are held and played correctly in the manner of the time.

JOHANNES VERMEER   1632 – 1675

Vermeer apparently spent his whole life in Delft, where he joined the painters' guild in 1653. He was influenced by the Delft painters de Hoogh and Carel Fabritius, as well as by the Caravaggesque painters of Utrecht. Although Vermeer painted relatively little and sold very few works, his pictures seem to have brought high prices. His reputation faded into total obscurity in the eighteenth century, and he was rediscovered only in the 1860s.

Officer and Laughing Girl   (11.1.127)

> Oil, on canvas, 19⅞ x 18⅛ in. (50.5 x 46 cm.). Painted perhaps 1655–60.
>
> COLLECTIONS: Double; Demidoff; Joseph; Knoedler; Frick (1911).

In what appears to be one of the first works of his maturity, Vermeer transforms the theme of girls entertaining their suitors, already a popular subject in Holland, into a remarkable study of light-filled space and of surfaces suffused with light. He pointedly contrasts the matte texture and dark tonality of the officer's silhouette with the bright, jewel-like effects of light on the costume and flesh of the girl. In Vermeer's later works such contrasts become more subtle, and the treatment of light still more adventurous. The map of Holland in the background of this painting was published in 1621 and appears in several of Vermeer's compositions.

Girl Interrupted at Her Music   (01.1.125)

> Oil, on canvas, 15½ x 17½ in. (39.3 x 44.4 cm.). Painted about 1660.
>
> COLLECTIONS: de Smeth-van Alphen; de Vries; Croese; Roos; Brondgeest; Woodburn; Gibson; Fry; Lawrie; Knoedler; Frick (1901).

Music-making, associated in the seventeenth century with courtship, figures prominently in Vermeer's interior scenes. Here he represents a duet which appears to have been momentarily interrupted. The picture of Cupid hanging on the wall is based on a popular seventeenth-century engraving symbolizing amorous fidelity.

VERMEER

Mistress and Maid   (19.1.126)

Oil, on canvas, 35½ x 31 in. (92 x 78.7 cm.). Painted perhaps 1665–70.

COLLECTIONS: Lebrun; Chevallier; Paillet; de Berri; Dufour; Secrétan; Sedelmeyer; Paulovtsof; Lawrie; Sulley; Simon; Knoedler; Frick (1919).

This late painting is exceptional among Vermeer's works in that it employs a simple curtained background in place of the numerous details customarily found in his interior scenes. The artist seldom surpassed the delicate soft-focus effects of light that are seen here on the mistress' pearls and the objects on the table. The lack of final modeling in the face and figure of the mistress indicates that Vermeer left the picture unfinished.

PAOLO CALIARI (IL VERONESE)
c. 1528 – 1588

Paolo Caliari was called Il Veronese after his birthplace, Verona. Except for a visit to Rome, he passed most of his mature life in and around Venice. He painted frescoes and altarpieces for churches and decorations for the villas of patrician families.

Allegory of Wisdom and Strength   (12.1.128)

Oil, on canvas, 84½ x 65¾ in. (214.6 x 167 cm.).

COLLECTIONS: Emperor Rudolph II; Queen Christina of Sweden; Azzolini; Odescalchi; d'Orléans; Walkeurs; Laborde-Méréville; Bridgewater with Gower and Carlisle; Hope; Agnew; Knoedler; Frick (1912).

Veronese's sumptuous style belies the moralizing theme of this picture: the triumph of celestial values over worldly interests. The female figure most likely personifies Divine Wisdom, with the traditional attribute of a sun over her head, while the powerful, somnolent male figure probably is meant to represent Hercules as an image of worldly power. Though this painting and its companion, *The Choice of Hercules* (see following entry), were not

necessarily executed as pendants, they have been together at least since 1621, when they were recorded in the possession of the Emperor Rudolph II. They have since passed together through some of the most famous European collections, among them those of Queen Christina of Sweden and the Duc d'Orléans.

VERONESE

Allegory of Virtue and Vice
(The Choice of Hercules)   (12.1.129)

Oil, on canvas, 86¼ x 66¾ in. (219 x 169.5 cm.).

COLLECTIONS: See preceding entry.

The theme of the Choice of Hercules was highly popular in Renaissance art and literature. According to the legend, Hercules resists the seductive embodiment of Vice, who offers him a life of ease and pleasure, and follows instead Virtue, who indicates a rugged lifelong ascent that, through toil and effort, will lead to true happiness. The motto on the entablature, "[HO]NOR ET VIRTUS / [P]OST MORTĒ FLORET" (Honor and Virtue Flourish after Death), reinforces the moral significance of the subject. Because of the distinctive physiognomy and elegant sixteenth-century clothing of the hero, the picture has often been considered an allegorizing portrait of the artist.

JAMES ABBOTT McNEILL WHISTLER
1834 – 1903

Born in Lowell, Massachusetts, Whistler spent part of his child-hood and most of his mature life in Europe. After three years at the West Point Military Academy, he went to London and then to Paris. He exhibited in the Salon des Refusés in 1863, and throughout his career he associated with his more experimental contemporaries. His wit as well as his advanced style of paint-ing frequently involved him in lively controversies.

The Ocean   (14.1.135)

> Oil, on canvas, 31¾ x 40⅛ in. (80.7 x 101.9 cm.). Signed with the butterfly monogram. Painted in 1866.
>
> COLLECTIONS: Taylor; Canfield; Knoedler; Frick (1914).

This painting, which was exhibited in London in 1892 as *Sym-phony in Grey and Green: The Ocean,* was one of several sea-scapes Whistler painted in 1866 during a visit to Valparaiso, Chile. The artist's adaptation of elements from Japanese wood-cuts is apparent here in the high horizon, the decorative ar-rangement of the bamboo sprays, and the cartouche at lower right. Both picture and frame — the latter designed by Whistler himself — bear the artist's characteristic butterfly monogram.

WHISTLER

Mrs. Frederick R. Leyland

(16.1.133)

Oil, on canvas, 77⅛ x 40¼ in. (195.9 x 102.2 cm.). Signed with the
butterfly monogram. Painted 1872–73.

COLLECTIONS: Leyland; Princep; Creelman; Frick (1916).

Frances Dawson (1834–1910) was the wife of Frederick R.
Leyland, a Liverpool shipowner who was one of Whistler's
chief patrons before they quarreled bitterly. The artist painted
the famous Peacock Room (now in the Freer Gallery, Washington) for the Leyland home in London. The Frick portrait,
originally entitled *Symphony in Flesh Colour and Pink*, apparently was never completely finished. The various preparatory
drawings for it are nearly all studies for Mrs. Leyland's gown,
which Whistler himself designed.

WHISTLER

Miss Rosa Corder (14.1.134)

Oil, on canvas, 75¾ x 36⅜ in. (192.4 x 92.4 cm.). Painted 1875–78.
COLLECTIONS: Howell; Robertson; Canfield; Knoedler; Frick (1914).

Rosa Corder, an artist, was a friend of Whistler's. It is said that Whistler observed her one day wearing a brown dress and passing before a black door and, struck by the subtle color effect, used it as a basis for this portrait, originally entitled *Arrangement in Black and Brown*. From contemporary remarks it would seem that the picture was already very dark at an early date; a letter written by Whistler suggests that he attempted to restore it in 1903.

WHISTLER

Valerie, Lady Meux (18.1.132)

Oil, on canvas, 76¼ x 36⅝ in. (193.7 x 93 cm.). Signed with the
butterfly monogram. Painted in 1881.
COLLECTIONS: Meux; Frick (1918/19).

Valerie Susie Reece (c.1856–1910) was the wife of Sir Henry
Bruce Meux, Bart., a brewer. An independent and colorful
figure in London society, she once appeared at a hunt riding
an elephant. This portrait is the second of three depictions of
Lady Meux that Whistler undertook, and was originally exhibited as *Harmony in Pink and Gray*. The first portrait — *Arrangement in Black and White* — is in the Honolulu Academy
of Arts; the third apparently was never finished.

WHISTLER

Robert, Comte de Montesquiou-Fezensac (14.1.131)

Oil, on canvas, 82⅛ x 36⅛ in. (208.6 x 91.8 cm.). Signed with the butterfly monogram. Painted 1891–92.

COLLECTIONS: de Montesquiou-Fezensac; Canfield; Knoedler; Frick (1914).

Robert, Comte de Montesquiou-Fezensac (1855–1921), was a prominent figure in the social and intellectual world of Paris around 1900. Though he published numerous volumes of poetry, he is probably best remembered today as one of the models for the character of the Baron de Charlus in Proust's *Remembrance of Things Past*. Whistler began two portraits of Montesquiou but finished only this one, originally entitled *Arrangement in Black and Gold*.

PHILIPS WOUWERMAN 1619 – 1668

Wouwerman was born in Haarlem, where he joined the painters' guild in 1640. His style was evidently much influenced by the genre paintings of Pieter van Laer ("Il Bamboccio"). Wouwerman's work was extremely popular in his own time and throughout the eighteenth century.

The Cavalry Camp (01.1.136)

Oil, on oak panel, 16¾ x 20¾ in. (42.5 x 52.7 cm.).
COLLECTIONS: Dinet; van Winter (?); van Loon; de Rothschild; Bösch; Bourgeois; Knoedler; Frick (1901).

Although Wouwerman seems to have spent most of his life in Haarlem, his numerous military scenes suggest that he traveled to observe Dutch border campaigns or foreign wars. His subtle sense of color and texture is evident in this composition, which anticipates the rococo tastes of the following century. Watteau's early military scenes, in particular, seem to depend upon precedents such as this.

INDEX OF ARTISTS

INDEX OF ARTISTS